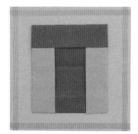

SHARE ON SOCIAL MEDIA!

When you create the pieces featured in this book, please feel free to post photos on Instagram, Facebook, Twitter and other social media platforms! Let's share the fun of handmade creations — such as what you've made, worn, or given as gifts with everyone. Use the #tuttleorigami hashtag to connect with other users, and mention @tuttleorigami so we can see and share your work!

Published by Tuttle Publishing, an imprint of Periplus Editions (HK) Ltd.

www.tuttlepublishing.com

978-4-8053-1788-4

ABC ORIGAMI (S8148)
Copyright © Boutique-sha, Inc. 2021
English translation rights arranged with Boutique-sha, Inc.
through Japan UNI Agency, Inc., Tokyo

All rights reserved. The items (text, photographs, drawings, etc.) included in this book are solely for personal use, and may not be reproduced for commercial purposes without permission of the copyright holders.

English translation © 2023 Periplus Editions (HK) Ltd
Translated from Japanese by Wendy Uchimura

Printed in China   2310EP
28 27 26 25 24   10 9 8 7 6 5 4 3 2 1

Distributed by:
North America, Latin America & Europe
Tuttle Publishing
364 Innovation Drive, North Clarendon, VT 05759-9436 USA
Tel: (802) 773-8930 | Fax: (802) 773-6993
info@tuttlepublishing.com | www.tuttlepublishing.com

Japan
Tuttle Publishing
Yaekari Building 3rd Floor,
5-4-12 Osaki Shinagawa-ku,Tokyo 141 0032
Tel: (81) 3 5437-0171 | Fax: (81) 3 5437-0755
sales@tuttle.co.jp | www.tuttle.co.jp

Asia Pacific
Berkeley Books Pte. Ltd.
3 Kallang Sector, #04-01, Singapore 349278
Tel: (65) 6741-2178 | Fax: (65) 6741-2179
inquiries@periplus.com.sg | www.tuttlepublishing.com

TUTTLE PUBLISHING® is a registered trademark of Tuttle Publishing, a division of Periplus Editions (HK) Ltd.

Fold Your Own Origami Alphabet!

This book can help you enjoy learning and memorizing the English alphabet. In just 4 steps, you can be an alphabet expert!

1. **First, learn how to fold the letters of the alphabet!**
2. **Next, try making the objects shown on the same page with the letters.**
3. **Think about the object's name while making each item.**
4. **Can you pronounce the word properly? Tell your friends about the words you've learned!**

Grown-ups

Using hands during play is great exercise for the brain and is said to improve cognitive and memory skills.

This is an educational origami book that encourages children to learn the alphabet while enjoying using their hands to make origami. The action of folding stimulates the brain, making a strong impression on a childís memory, and kids will enjoy being able to make letters of the alphabet and other items with their own hands. The completed pieces can be arranged and used in so many ways, such as to memorize words, create a personal ABC picture book (see page 113) or make a poster from panels of letters, like on the contents page, to help learn the alphabet. We hope this book will help to improve your child's English, as well as their memory and cognitive skills.

Apple

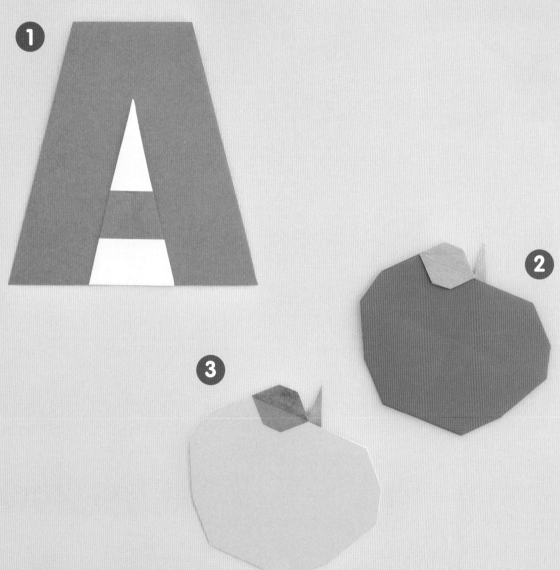

Folding Instructions

Bus

Folding Instructions

Cat

Folding Instructions

Donut

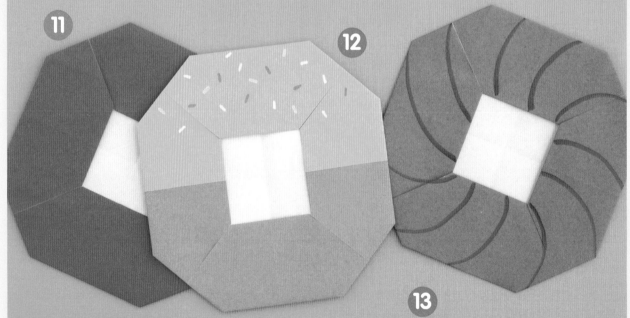

10

11

12

13

Elephant

Flower

⑰

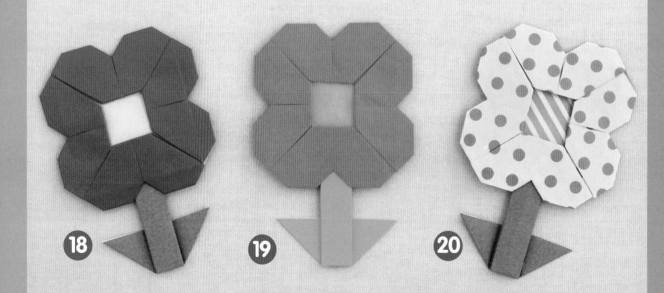

⑱   ⑲   ⑳

Folding Instructions

Girl

21

22

23

Folding Instructions

9

Hamburger

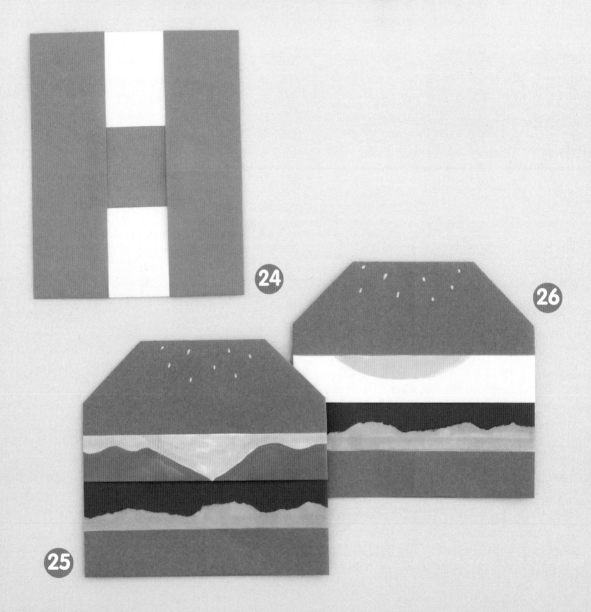

Folding Instructions

Ice cream

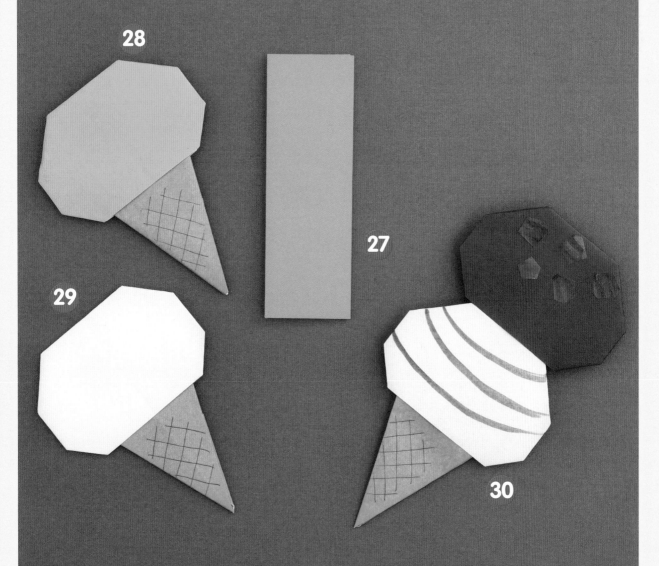

28

27

29

30

Folding Instructions

Juice

Folding Instructions

Key

Folding Instructions

Ladybug

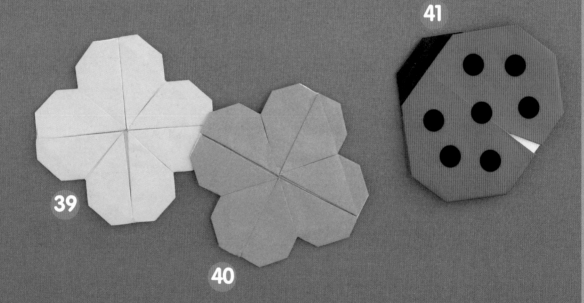

38

41

39

40

Music

Nice

Folding Instructions

Owl

Folding Instructions

Pencil

52

53

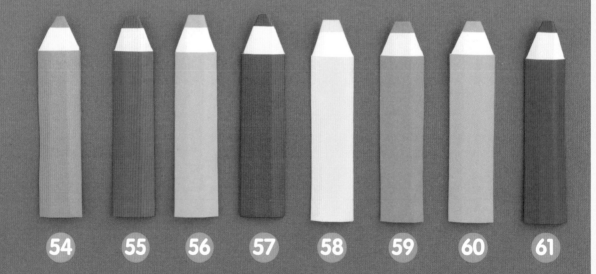

54 55 56 57 58 59 60 61

Folding Instructions

Queen

Rice

68

69

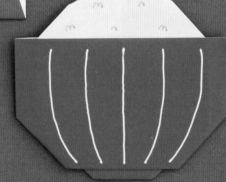

70

Folding Instructions

Strawberry

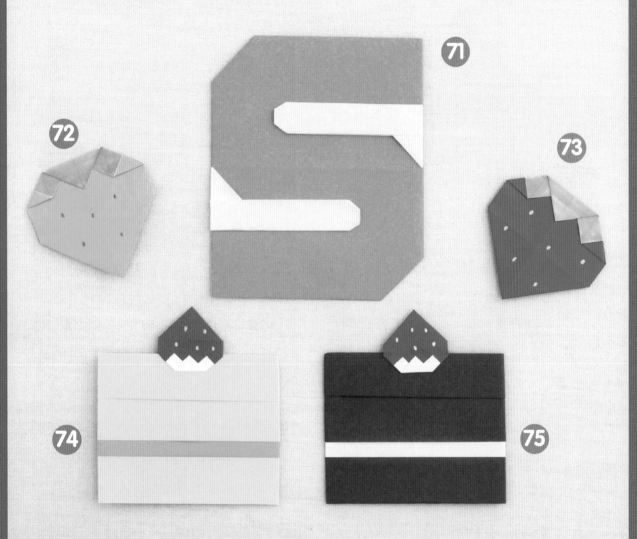

Folding Instructions

Tree

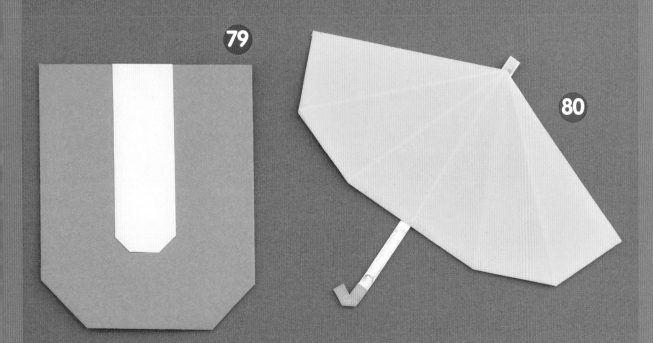

Umbrella

Violin

82

83

84

85

Watch

86

87

88

Folding Instructions

Box

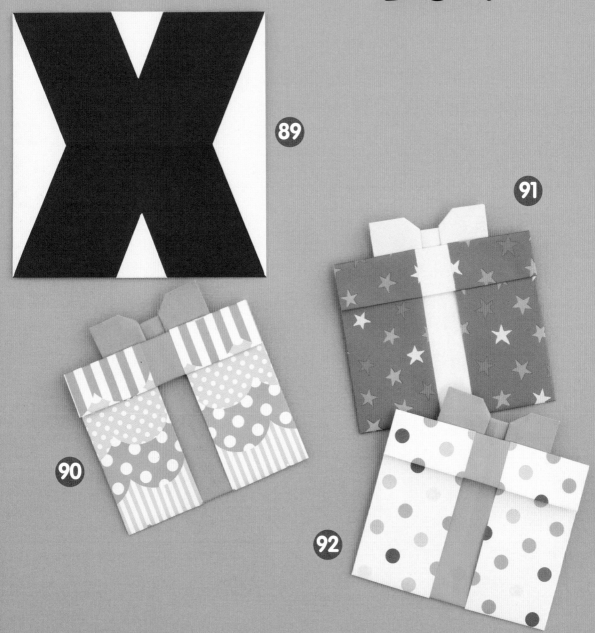

Folding Instructions

Yacht

Folding Instructions

Zebra

Folding Instructions

How to Fold Numbers

Here, we look at numbers. Have fun mixing and matching them with the letters of the alphabet. This will expand your world of ABC Origami.

Fun Ways to Customize Your Origami

Use letters of the alphabet to create special messages!

HAPPY BIRTHDAY

Glue the initials of everyone's names on a paper cup

Customizing Example 2

Birthday Party

Use handmade items to make this a very special party!

Customization Techniques

With just a few small adjustments these letters will look even more special! Here are a number of techniques that you can use to customize your pieces.

Technique 1

Just line up the folded letters and you can make words!

Technique 2

Use double-sided origami paper and glue the letter panel onto like-colored backgrounds!

Technique 3

Glue them to construction paper and cut around them to create a border!

Technique 4

Combine words with folded origami models!

Make it even more special

Glue the items you've folded onto origami paper to create a cute panel! All of the letters on the Contents pages are panels like this.

Before You Begin

Here is some information you should become familiar with in order to understand the folding sequences in this book. First, learn how to fold two simple bases, and review the meanings of arrows, marks and symbols. Then, begin folding origami!

Base Folds Used in This Book

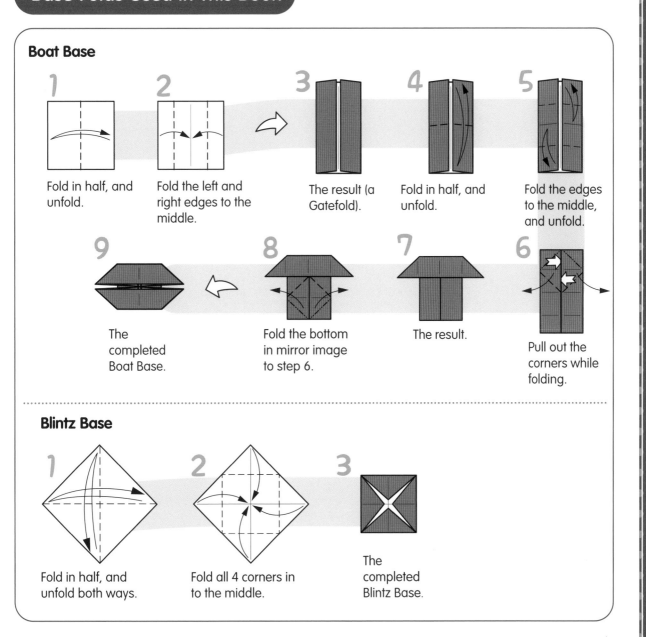

Boat Base

1. Fold in half, and unfold.

2. Fold the left and right edges to the middle.

3. The result (a Gatefold).

4. Fold in half, and unfold.

5. Fold the edges to the middle, and unfold.

6. Pull out the corners while folding.

7. The result.

8. Fold the bottom in mirror image to step 6.

9. The completed Boat Base.

Blintz Base

1. Fold in half, and unfold both ways.

2. Fold all 4 corners in to the middle.

3. The completed Blintz Base.

Instructions and Folds Used in This Book

Valley Fold
Fold so that the dotted line is on the inside.

- "Valley fold" line
- - - - - - - - - -

Valley fold arrow

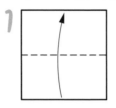

Mountain Fold
Fold so that the dotted line is on the outside.

- "Mountain fold" line
·–··–··–··–··–··–·

Mountain fold arrow

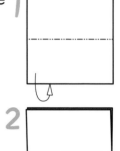

Make a Crease
Fold, and then unfold the paper.

- "Crease" indication

Fold and unfold arrow

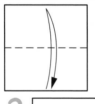

Open a Pocket
Insert your finger where the white arrow indicates to open a pocket.

- "Open a pocket" indication

Push open arrow

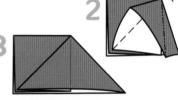

Flip Over
Flip horizontally, from left to right.

- "Flip" indication

Flip symbol

Flip

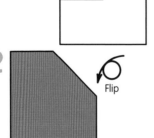

Flip

Rotate
Turn the paper clockwise or counterclockwise as indicated.

- "Rotate" indication

Rotate symbols

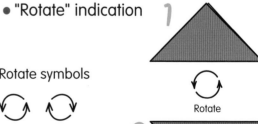
Rotate

Outside Reverse Fold

Pop a corner in the opposite direction, wrapping it outside.

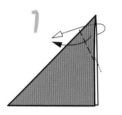

Inside Reverse Fold

Pop a corner in the opposite direction, tucking it inside.

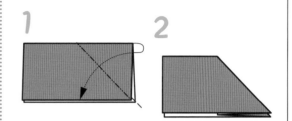

Insert

Tuck a tab into a pocket.

- "Insert" indication

Insert symbol

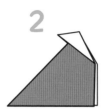

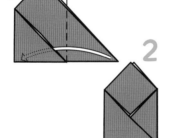

Zoom

The following illustration will be displayed larger or smaller than the previous one.

- "Zoom" indication

Zoom symbols

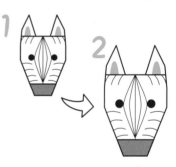

Equal Divisions

The indicated spans are each of equal length.

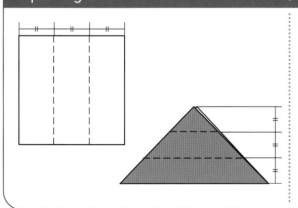

X-ray

Lines used to indicate the position of layers that are hidden by the top layer.

- "X-ray" line

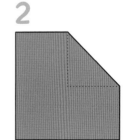

Materials

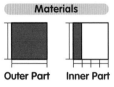

Outer Part | Inner Part

★ A (outer part)

Start with a Blintz Base (see page 33)

1

Fold the top corners to meet in the center. The creases should terminate at the circled locations.

2

The result.

Turn over

3

Completed.

★ A (inner part)

1

① Fold.
② Make a crease.

Make criss-crossing central creases and then:
① Fold.
② Make a crease.

2

Fold up twice.

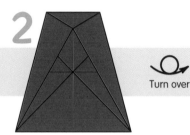

3

The result.

Turn over

4

Fold the corners to the center.

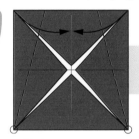

All Done!

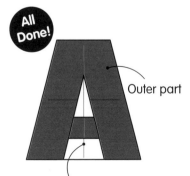

Outer part

Inner part

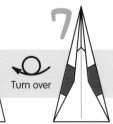

8

Completed.

7

Turn over

The result.

6

Fold in from corner to corner.

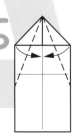

5

Fold the corners to the center.

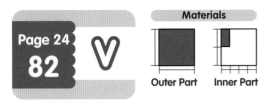

Materials

Outer Part   Inner Part

⭐ V (inner part)

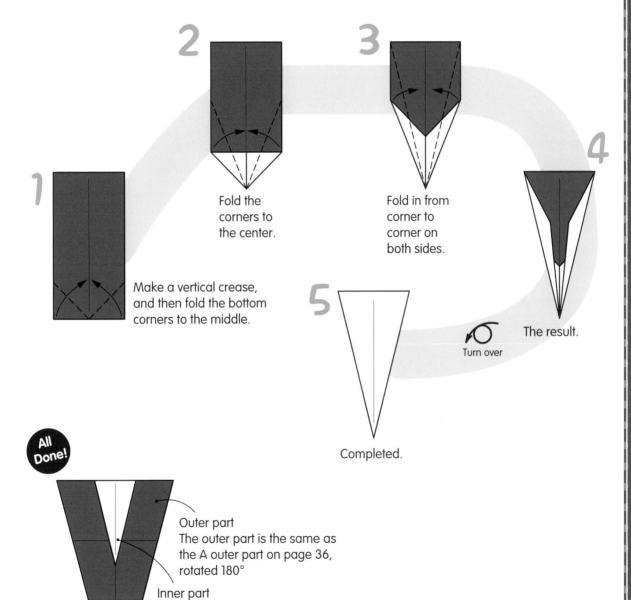

2
Fold the corners to the center.

3
Fold in from corner to corner on both sides.

4
The result.

1
Make a vertical crease, and then fold the bottom corners to the middle.

Turn over

5
Completed.

All Done!

Outer part
The outer part is the same as the A outer part on page 36, rotated 180°

Inner part

Materials

Outer Part   Opening × 2

⭐ A (outer part)

Start with a Blintz Base (see page 33)

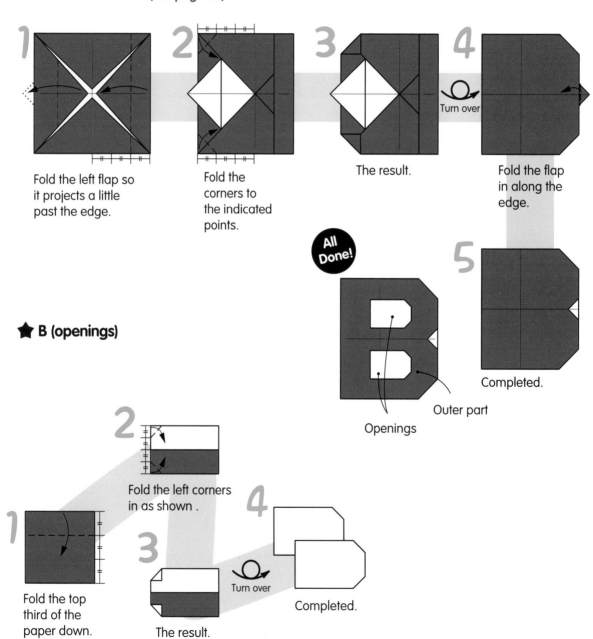

1 Fold the left flap so it projects a little past the edge.

2 Fold the corners to the indicated points.

3 The result.

4 Turn over

Fold the flap in along the edge.

5 Completed.

All Done!

Openings

Outer part

⭐ B (openings)

1 Fold the top third of the paper down.

2 Fold the left corners in as shown.

3 Turn over

The result.

4 Completed.

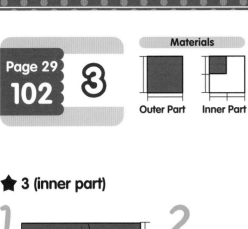

Materials

Outer Part   Inner Part

⭐ **3 (inner part)**

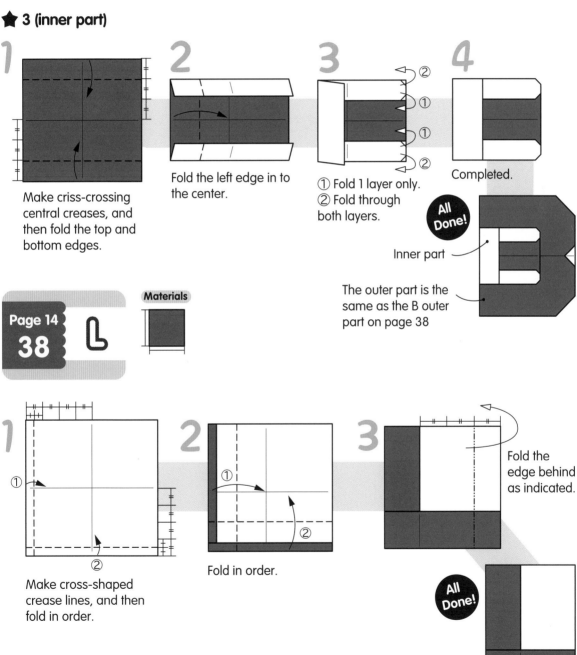

1
Make criss-crossing central creases, and then fold the top and bottom edges.

2
Fold the left edge in to the center.

3
① Fold 1 layer only.
② Fold through both layers.

4
Completed.

All Done!

Inner part

The outer part is the same as the B outer part on page 38

Page 14
38

Materials

1
Make cross-shaped crease lines, and then fold in order.

2
Fold in order.

3
Fold the edge behind as indicated.

All Done!

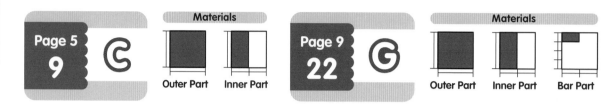

Page 5
9

Page 9
22

Materials

Outer Part | Inner Part

Materials

Outer Part | Inner Part | Bar Part

★ C • G (outer part)

Start with a Blintz Base (see page 33)

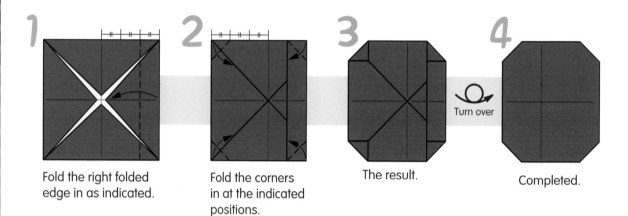

1
Fold the right folded edge in as indicated.

2
Fold the corners in at the indicated positions.

3
The result.

Turn over

4
Completed.

★ C • G (inner part)

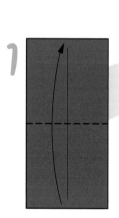

1
Make a vertical crease in the middle, and then fold in half.

2
Make a crease line only on the top layer.

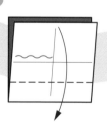

3
Fold so the crease indicated by the wavy line aligns with the bottom.

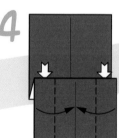

4
Fold the left and right edges of the flap to the center. Collapse the paper that flares at the top into triangles.

★ G (bar part)

1

Make a vertical crease in the middle, and then fold up the bottom edge at the indicated position.

2

Fold the right edge to the middle .

3

The result.

4

Turn over

Completed.

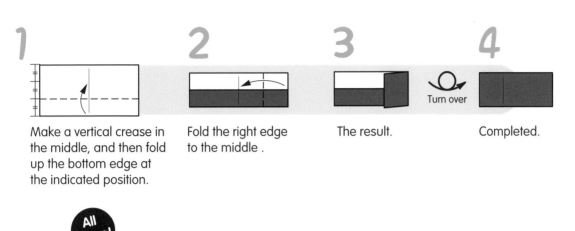

All Done!

C • G (outer part)   C • G (inner part)

C•G (outer part)

G (bar part)

C • G (inner part)

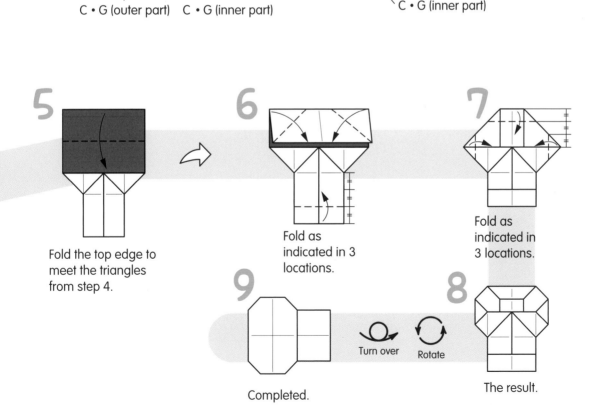

5

Fold the top edge to meet the triangles from step 4.

6

Fold as indicated in 3 locations.

7

Fold as indicated in 3 locations.

9

Turn over   Rotate

Completed.

8

The result.

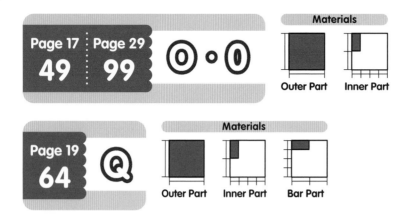

Materials

Outer Part   Inner Part

Materials

Outer Part   Inner Part   Bar Part

★ O • 0 (inner part)

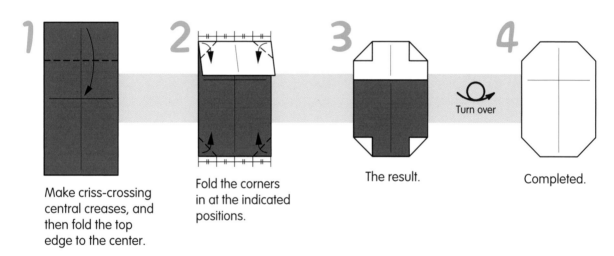

1 Make criss-crossing central creases, and then fold the top edge to the center.

2 Fold the corners in at the indicated positions.

3 The result.

Turn over

4 Completed.

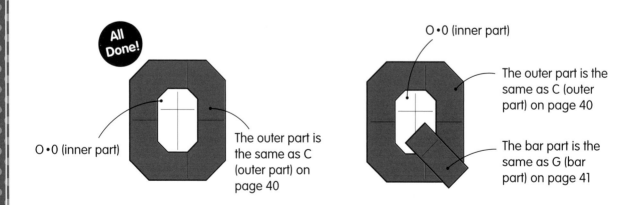

All Done!

O•0 (inner part)

O•0 (inner part)

The outer part is the same as C (outer part) on page 40

O•0 (inner part)

The outer part is the same as C (outer part) on page 40

The bar part is the same as G (bar part) on page 41

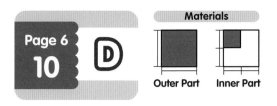
Materials

Outer Part   Inner Part

⭐ D (outer part)

Start with a Blintz Base (see page 33)

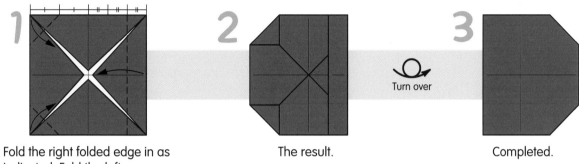

1 Fold the right folded edge in as indicated. Fold the left corners in at the indicated positions.

2 The result.

Turn over

3 Completed.

⭐ D (inner part)

Start with a Blintz Base (see page 33)

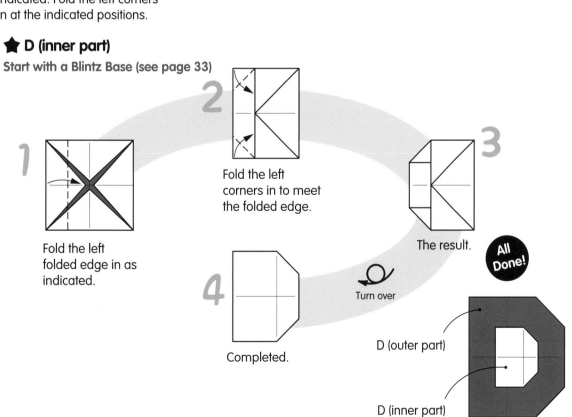

1 Fold the left folded edge in as indicated.

2 Fold the left corners in to meet the folded edge.

3 The result.

All Done!

4 Completed.

Turn over

D (outer part)

D (inner part)

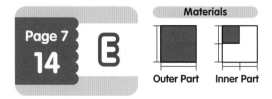

Materials

Outer Part   Inner Part

⭐ E (outer part)

Start with a Blintz Base (see page 33)

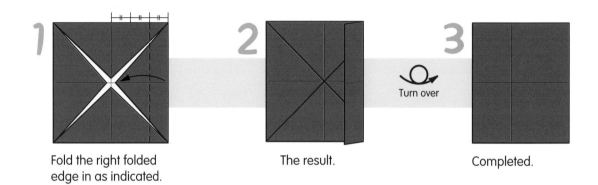

1 Fold the right folded edge in as indicated.

2 The result.

Turn over

3 Completed.

⭐ E (inner part)

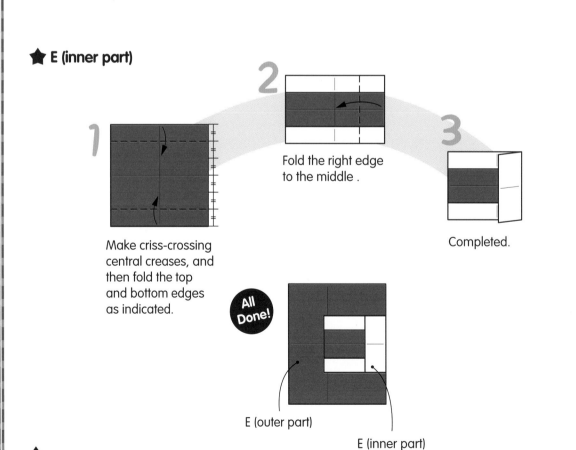

1 Make criss-crossing central creases, and then fold the top and bottom edges as indicated.

2 Fold the right edge to the middle.

3 Completed.

All Done!

E (outer part)

E (inner part)

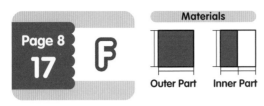

Materials

Outer Part   Inner Part

⭐ F (inner part)

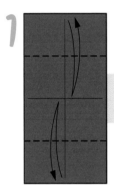

Make criss-crossing central creases, and then fold and unfold the top and bottom edges to the center.

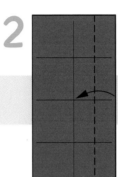

Fold the right edge to the middle.

Fold the top edge to the crease. Fold and unfold the bottom edge.

Completed.

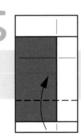

Fold the bottom edge up on the existing crease.

Fold the top and bottom edges as indicated.

All Done!

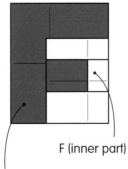

F (inner part)

The outer part is the same as E (outer part) on page 44

Materials

Outer Part Inner Part x 2

⭐ **N (inner parts)**

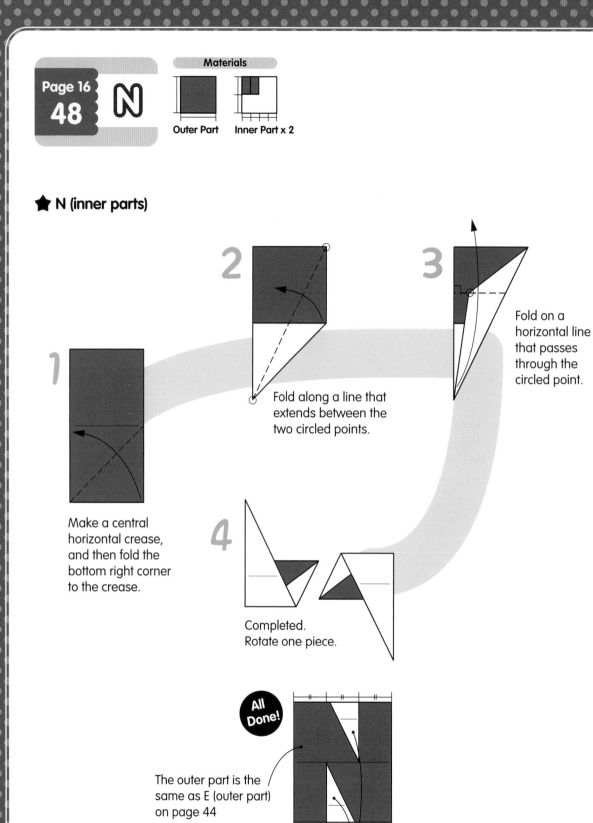

1 Make a central horizontal crease, and then fold the bottom right corner to the crease.

2 Fold along a line that extends between the two circled points.

3 Fold on a horizontal line that passes through the circled point.

4 Completed. Rotate one piece.

All Done!

The outer part is the same as E (outer part) on page 44

Sandwich the outer part with N (inner parts)

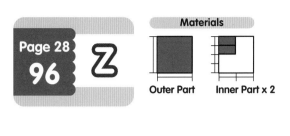

Materials

Outer Part   Inner Part x 2

★ Z (inner parts)

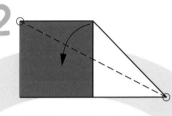

2

Fold along a line that extends between the two circled points.

1

Make a central vertical crease, and then fold the top right corner to the crease.

3

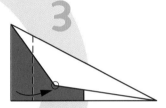

Fold the left edge so that it meets the circled point.

5

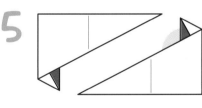

Completed.

Turn over

4

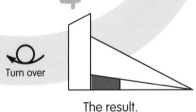

The result.

★ Z (outer part)

From step 3 of E (outer part) (see page 44)

Z (inner part)

1

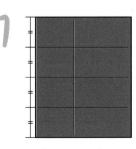

Make crease lines.

All Done!

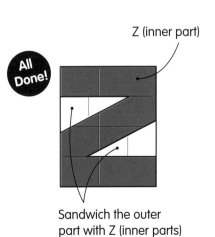

Sandwich the outer part with Z (inner parts)

Page 12
34

Page 23
79

Materials

Outer Part   Inner Part

Materials

Outer Part   Inner Part

★ J • U (outer part)
Start with a Blintz Base (see page 33)

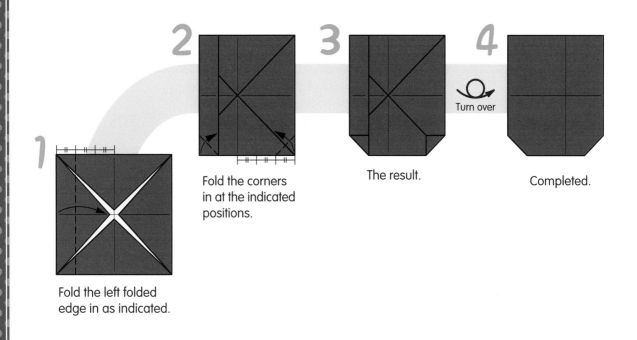

1 Fold the left folded edge in as indicated.

2 Fold the corners in at the indicated positions.

3 The result.

Turn over

4 Completed.

★ U (inner part)

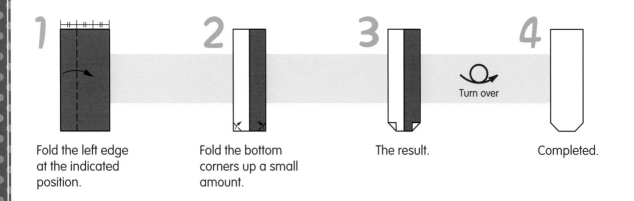

1 Fold the left edge at the indicated position.

2 Fold the bottom corners up a small amount.

3 The result.

Turn over

4 Completed.

⭐ J (inner part)

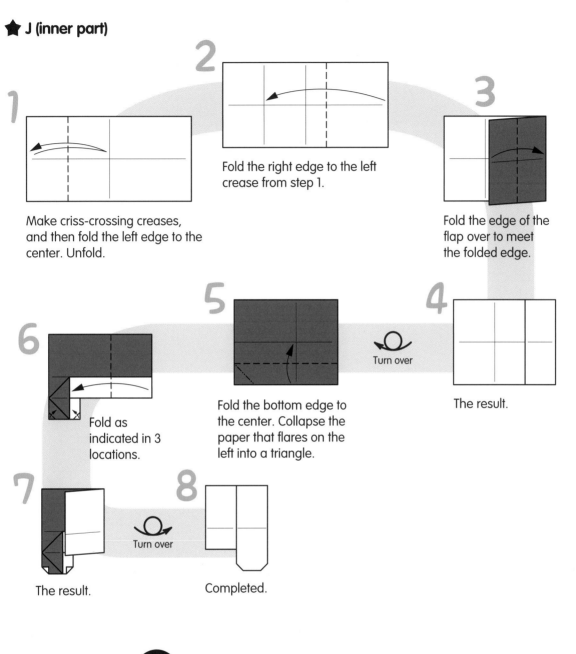

1 Make criss-crossing creases, and then fold the left edge to the center. Unfold.

2 Fold the right edge to the left crease from step 1.

3 Fold the edge of the flap over to meet the folded edge.

4 The result.

Turn over

5 Fold the bottom edge to the center. Collapse the paper that flares on the left into a triangle.

6 Fold as indicated in 3 locations.

7 The result.

Turn over

8 Completed.

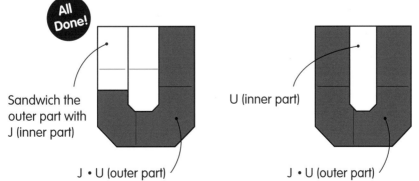

All Done!

Sandwich the outer part with J (inner part)

J • U (outer part)

U (inner part)

J • U (outer part)

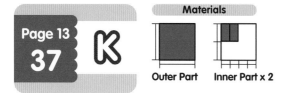

Materials

Outer Part Inner Part x 2

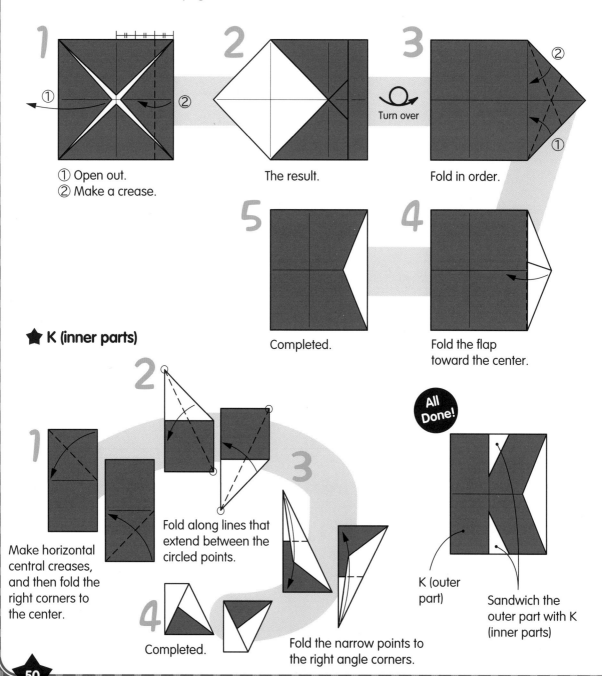

⭐ K (outer part)

Start with a Blintz Base (see page 33)

1
① Open out.
② Make a crease.

2
The result.

Turn over

3
Fold in order.

4
Fold the flap toward the center.

5
Completed.

⭐ K (inner parts)

1
Make horizontal central creases, and then fold the right corners to the center.

2
Fold along lines that extend between the circled points.

3
Fold the narrow points to the right angle corners.

4
Completed.

All Done!

K (outer part)

Sandwich the outer part with K (inner parts)

50

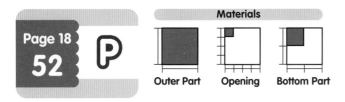

Materials

Outer Part　　Opening　　Bottom Part

⭐ P (outer part)

Start with a Blintz Base (see page 33)

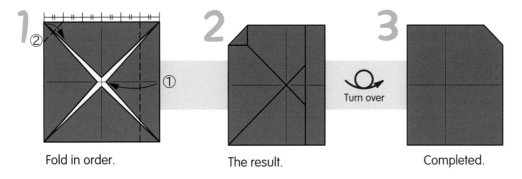

1 Fold in order.

2 The result.

Turn over

3 Completed.

⭐ P (bottom part)

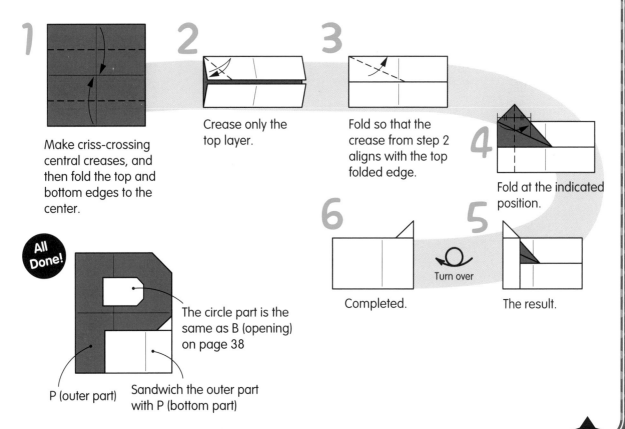

1 Make criss-crossing central creases, and then fold the top and bottom edges to the center.

2 Crease only the top layer.

3 Fold so that the crease from step 2 aligns with the top folded edge.

4 Fold at the indicated position.

5 The result.

Turn over

6 Completed.

All Done!

The circle part is the same as B (opening) on page 38

P (outer part)

Sandwich the outer part with P (bottom part)

Page 11
27

Materials

Page 29
100

Materials

★ I • 1

Start with a Blintz Base (see page 33)

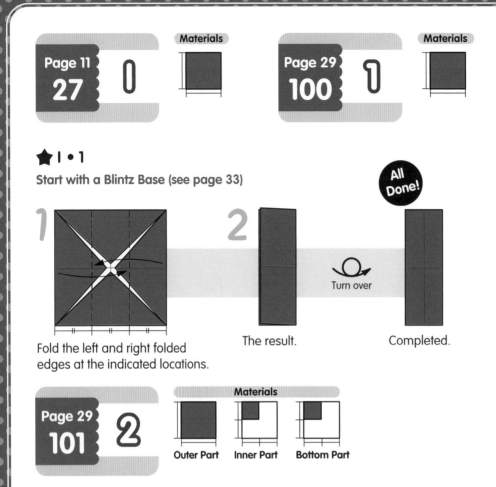

1 Fold the left and right folded edges at the indicated locations.

2 The result.

Turn over

All Done!

Completed.

Page 29
101

Materials

Outer Part   Inner Part   Bottom Part

★ 2 (top part • bottom part)

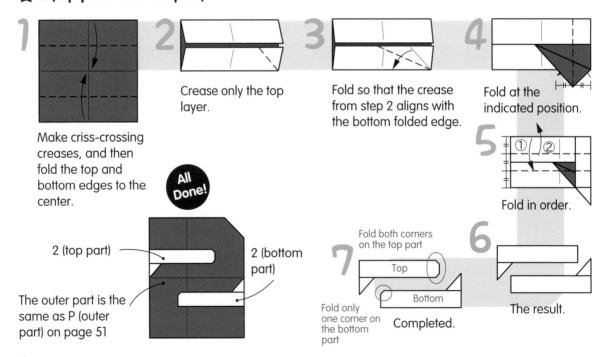

1 Make criss-crossing creases, and then fold the top and bottom edges to the center.

2 Crease only the top layer.

3 Fold so that the crease from step 2 aligns with the bottom folded edge.

4 Fold at the indicated position.

5 ① ② Fold in order.

6 The result.

7 Fold both corners on the top part
Top
Bottom
Fold only one corner on the bottom part
Completed.

All Done!

2 (top part)

2 (bottom part)

The outer part is the same as P (outer part) on page 51

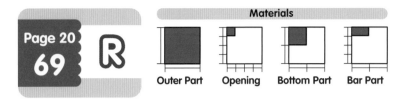

Materials

Outer Part | Opening | Bottom Part | Bar Part

⭐ R (bar part)

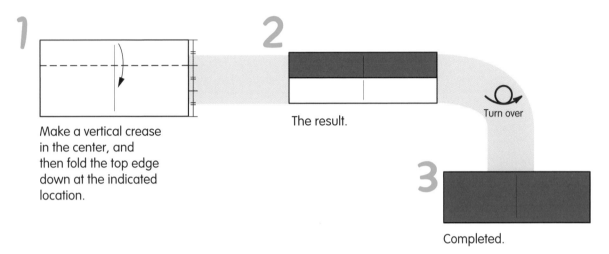

1 Make a vertical crease in the center, and then fold the top edge down at the indicated location.

2 The result.

Turn over

3 Completed.

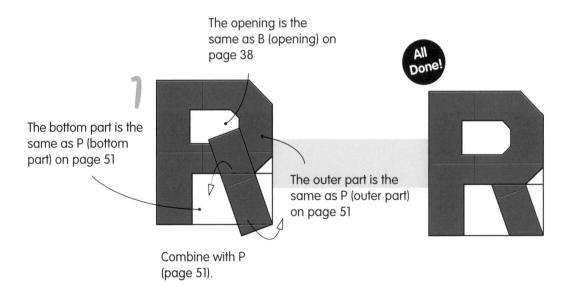

The opening is the same as B (opening) on page 38

1

All Done!

The bottom part is the same as P (bottom part) on page 51

The outer part is the same as P (outer part) on page 51

Combine with P (page 51).

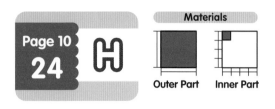

Materials

Outer Part · Inner Part

★ H (outer part)

1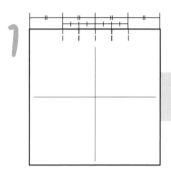

Make criss-crossing central creases, and then install pinch lines at the edge of the paper at the indicated locations.

2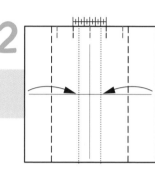

Fold at the indicated locations.

3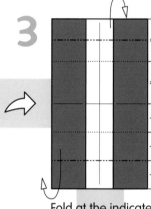

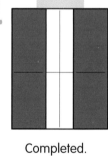

Fold at the indicated locations.

4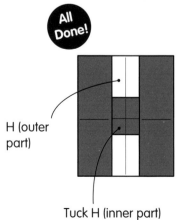

Completed.

★ H (inner part)

1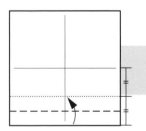

Make criss-crossing central creases, and then fold the bottom edge up at the indicated location.

2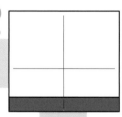

The result.

Turn over

3

Completed.

All Done!

H (outer part)

Tuck H (inner part) underneath the flaps

Materials

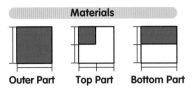

Outer Part   **Top Part**   **Bottom Part**

★ M (top part)

1
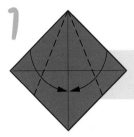

Make criss-crossing central diagonal creases, and then fold the upper sides to the center.

2

Fold top to bottom.

3

Completed.

★ (bottom part)

1
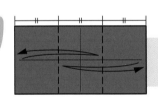

Make criss-crossing central creases, and then fold and unfold the left and right edges to the indicated locations.

2
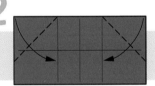

Fold the corners in, using the creases from step 1 as landmarks.

3
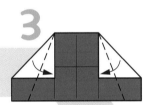

Fold to bisect the angles.

4
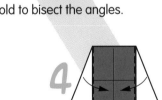

Fold in the flaps.

5

Fold the bottom half up behind.

6

Completed.

All Done!

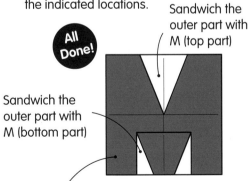

Sandwich the outer part with M (top part)

Sandwich the outer part with M (bottom part)

The outer part is the same as step 3 of the Blintz Base on page 33

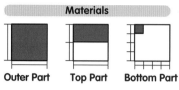

Materials

Outer Part   Top Part   Bottom Part

★ W (outer part)

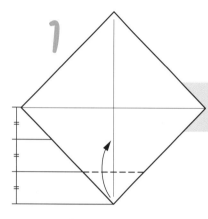

Make criss-crossing
diagonal central creases,
and then fold the bottom
corner up at the indicated
location.

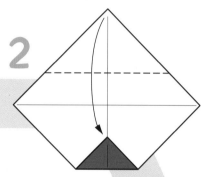

Fold the top corner down to meet
the top of the triangular bottom flap.

Fold the left and right corners in to lie
along the edges of the upper flap.

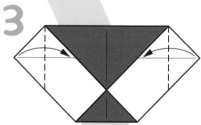

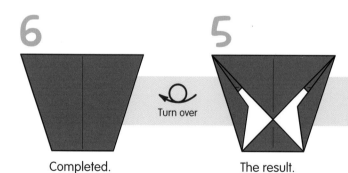

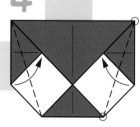

Fold along lines that
extend between the
circled points.

Completed.   The result.   Turn over

⭐ W (top part)

1

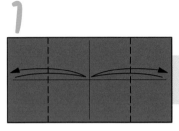

Make criss-crossing central creases, and then fold and unfold the left and right edges to the center.

2

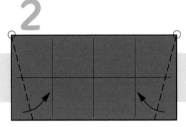

Fold the bottom corners in so they contact the outer creases from step 1.

3

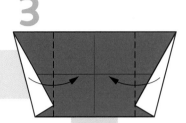

Fold the left and right flaps in on the creases from step 1.

6

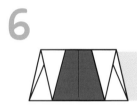

Completed.

5

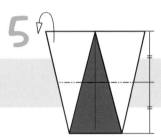

Fold the top half down behind.

4

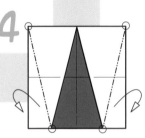

Fold behind on both sides along lines that extend between the circled points.

⭐ W (bottom part)

1

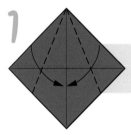

Make criss-crossing central diagonal creases, and then fold the upper sides to the center.

2

Fold the bottom triangular flap up.

3

The result.

Turn over

4

Completed.

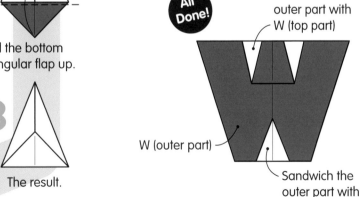

All Done!

Sandwich the outer part with W (top part)

W (outer part)

Sandwich the outer part with W (bottom part)

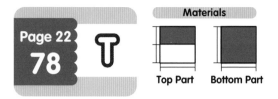

Materials

Top Part   Bottom Part

★ T (bottom part)

1 Make criss-crossing central creases, and then install pinch lines at the edge of the paper at the indicated locations.

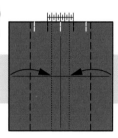

2 Fold at the indicated locations.

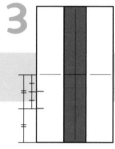

3 Install pinch lines at the edge of the paper at the indicated locations.

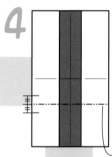

4 Fold behind along a line that falls between the pinch marks from step 3.

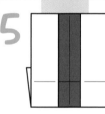

5

Completed.

★ T (top part)

1 Make criss-crossing central creases, and then fold the top edge down at the indicated location.

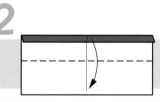

2 Fold the top portion down along the existing central crease.

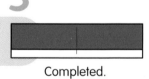

3

Completed.

★ Assembly

Make sure the crease lines meet up

All Done!

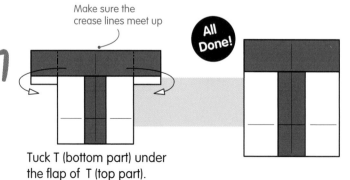

1 Tuck T (bottom part) under the flap of T (top part).

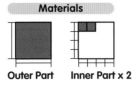

Materials

Outer Part   Inner Part x 2

⭐ X (outer part)

Start with a Blintz Base (see page 33)

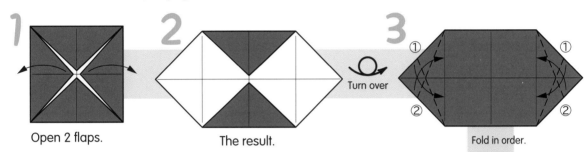

1 Open 2 flaps.

2 The result.

Turn over

3 ① ② Fold in order.

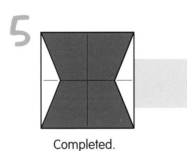

5 Completed.

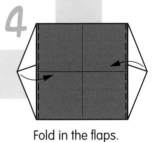

4 Fold in the flaps.

⭐ X (inner parts)

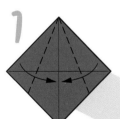

1 Make criss-crossing central diagonal creases, and then fold the upper sides to the center.

2 Fold top to bottom.

3 Completed.

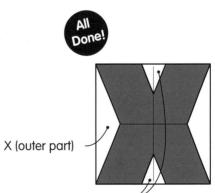

All Done!

X (outer part)

Sandwich the outer part with X (inner parts).

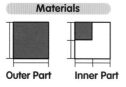

Outer Part   Inner Part

★ 4 (outer part)

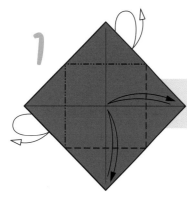

1. Make criss-crossing central diagonal creases, and then fold the flaps into the center in front and behind as shown.

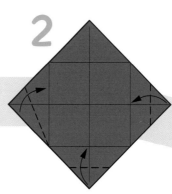

2. Fold as indicated in 3 locations.

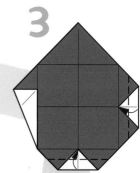

3. Continue folding the right and bottom flaps.

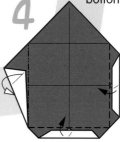

4. Continue folding the right and bottom flaps. Fold the left flap behind.

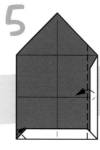

5. Fold the right flap over once more.

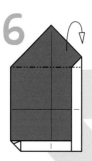

6. Fold the top portion behind.

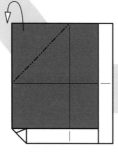

7. Fold the top right corner behind.

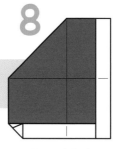

8. Completed.

⭐ 4 (inner part)

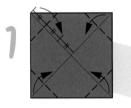

1 Make a cross-shaped crease line and then fold.

2

3 Completed.

Page 21
71 S

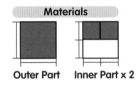

Materials

Outer Part   Inner Part x 2

⭐ S (outer part)

Start with a Blintz Base (see page 33)

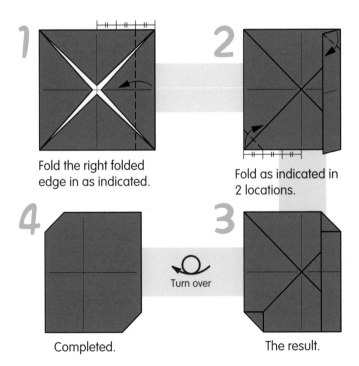

1 Fold the right folded edge in as indicated.

2 Fold as indicated in 2 locations.

Turn over

3 The result.

4 Completed.

⭐ Assembly

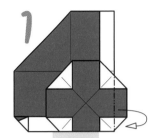

1 Superimpose 4 (inner part) on 4 (outer part) and fold the flap behind to finish.

All Done!

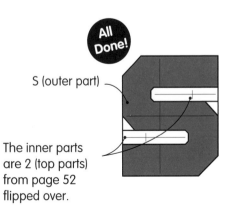

All Done!

S (outer part)

The inner parts are 2 (top parts) from page 52 flipped over.

Materials

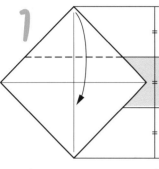

1

Make criss-crossing central diagonal creases, and then fold the top flap down as indicated.

2

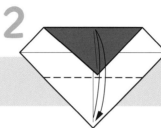

Make a crease.

3

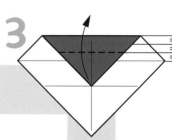

Fold the flap up.

4

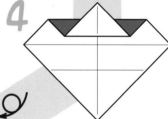

The result.

5

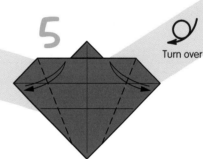
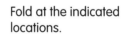

Turn over

Fold at the indicated locations.

6

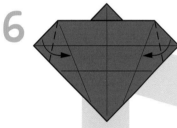
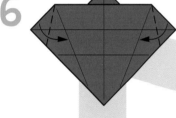

7

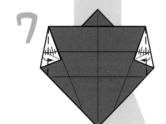

8

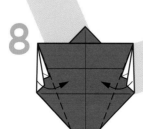

9

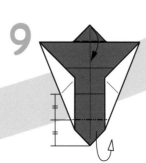

Fold behind.

All Done!

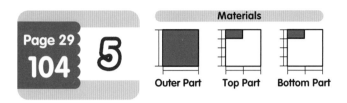

Materials

Outer Part   Top Part   Bottom Part

★ 5 (outer part)

Start with a Blintz Base (see page 33)

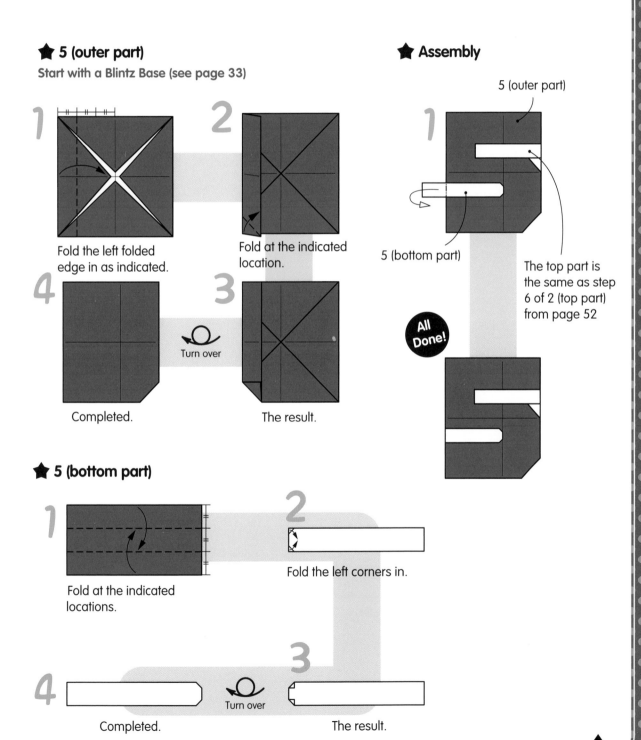

1 Fold the left folded edge in as indicated.

2 Fold at the indicated location.

3 The result.

Turn over

4 Completed.

★ 5 (bottom part)

1 Fold at the indicated locations.

2 Fold the left corners in.

3 The result.

Turn over

4 Completed.

★ Assembly

5 (outer part)

5 (bottom part)

The top part is the same as step 6 of 2 (top part) from page 52

All Done!

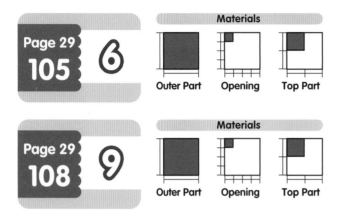

Materials

Page 29
105   6

Outer Part   Opening   Top Part

★ 6 • 9 (outer part)

Start with a Blintz Base (see page 33)

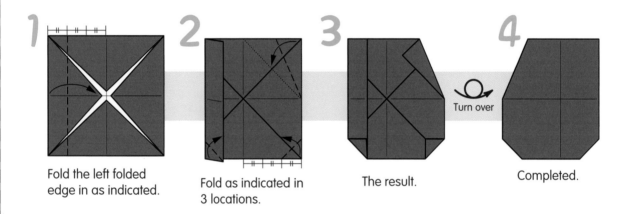

1 Fold the left folded edge in as indicated.

2 Fold as indicated in 3 locations.

3 The result.

Turn over

4 Completed.

★ 6 • 9 (opening)

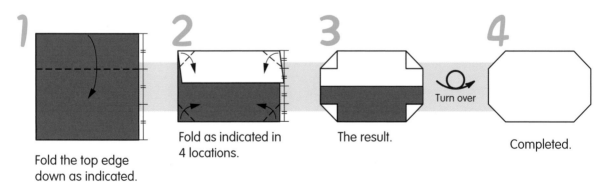

1 Fold the top edge down as indicated.

2 Fold as indicated in 4 locations.

3 The result.

Turn over

4 Completed.

★ 6 • 9 (top part)

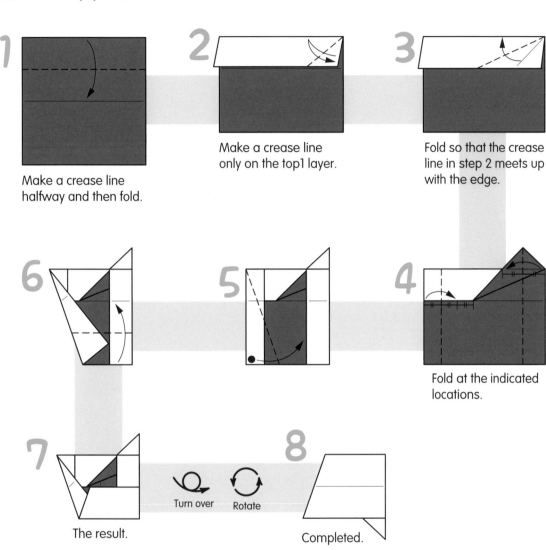

1 Make a crease line halfway and then fold.

2 Make a crease line only on the top1 layer.

3 Fold so that the crease line in step 2 meets up with the edge.

4 Fold at the indicated locations.

5

6

7 The result.

Turn over   Rotate

8 Completed.

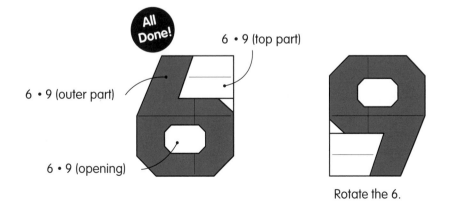

All Done!

6 • 9 (top part)

6 • 9 (outer part)

6 • 9 (opening)

Rotate the 6.

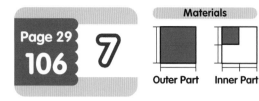

Materials

Outer Part   Inner Part

⭐ 7 (outer part)
Start with a Blintz Base (see page 33)

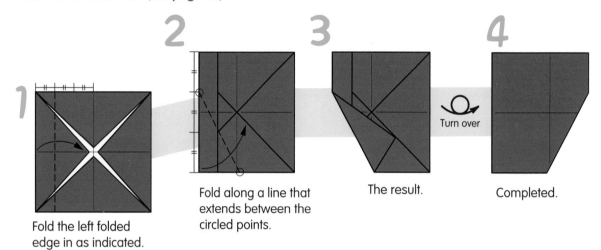

1 Fold the left folded edge in as indicated.

2 Fold along a line that extends between the circled points.

3 The result.

Turn over

4 Completed.

⭐ 7 (inner part)

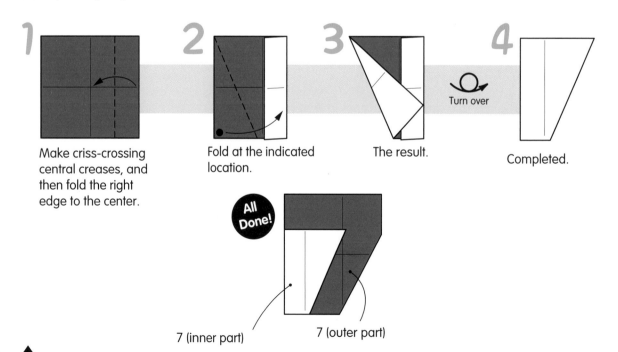

1 Make criss-crossing central creases, and then fold the right edge to the center.

2 Fold at the indicated location.

3 The result.

Turn over

4 Completed.

All Done!

7 (inner part)   7 (outer part)

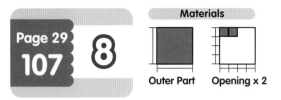

Materials

Outer Part   Opening x 2

★ 8 (outer part)

Start with a Blintz Base (see page 33)

1

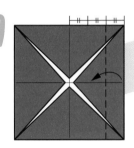

Fold the right folded edge in as indicated.

2

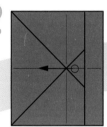

Pull out the corner marked.

3

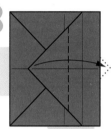

Fold the flap so it projects a little past the edge.

4

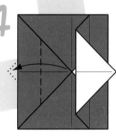

Fold the flap so it projects a little past the edge.

5

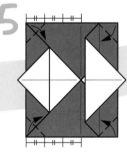

Fold at the indicated locations.

6

The result.

Turn over

7

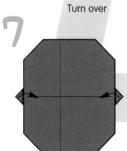

Fold the flaps in along the edge.

8

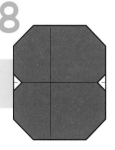

Completed.

All Done!

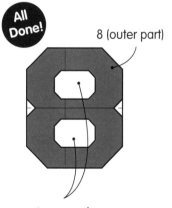

8 (outer part)

The openings are the same as 6•9 (opening) on page 64.

Page 29
109

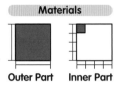

Materials

Outer Part   Inner Part

⭐ ! (outer part)

1

Make criss-crossing central creases, and then fold the bottom corners to the center.

2

Fold behind at the indicated location.

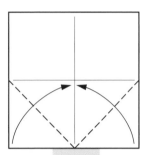

3

Fold in at the indicated locations.

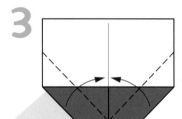

4

X-ray view of the bottom portion of the fold lines

6

Fold as indicated. The flaps will overlap.

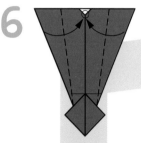

5

Fold behind and then tuck the triangular flaps into the pocket.

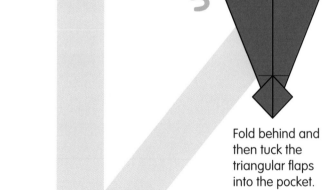

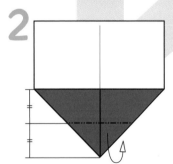

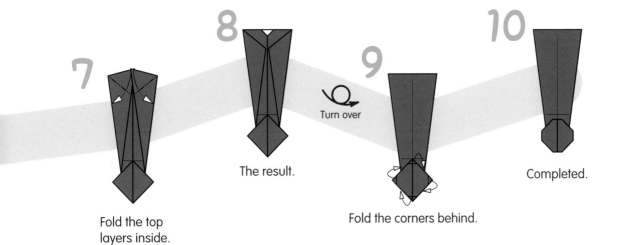

7

Fold the top layers inside.

8

The result.

Turn over

9

Fold the corners behind.

10

Completed.

⭐ **! (inner part)**

1

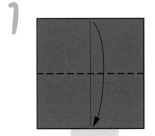

Make a vertical central crease, and then fold the paper in half, top to bottom.

2

Completed.

⭐ **Assembly**

1

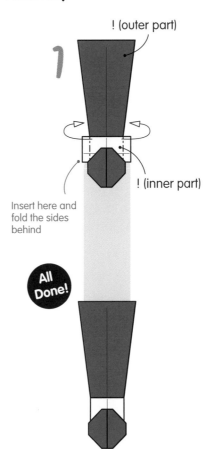

! (outer part)

! (inner part)

Insert here and fold the sides behind

All Done!

Cat

Materials

Face   Body

★ **Face**

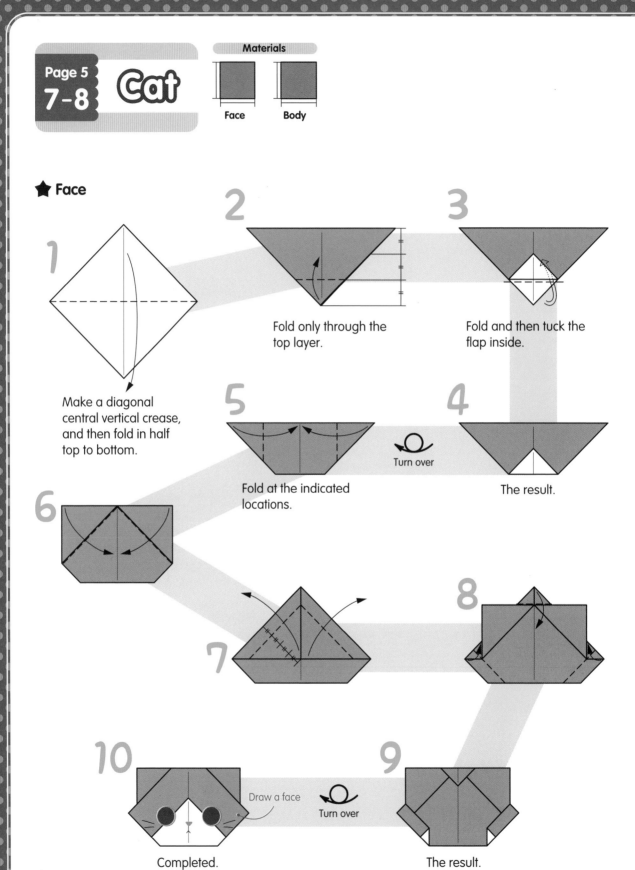

1
Make a diagonal central vertical crease, and then fold in half top to bottom.

2
Fold only through the top layer.

3
Fold and then tuck the flap inside.

4
The result.

Turn over

5
Fold at the indicated locations.

6

7

8

9
The result.

Turn over

10
Draw a face
Completed.

⭐ Body

(For 8, make sure to fold in mirror image)

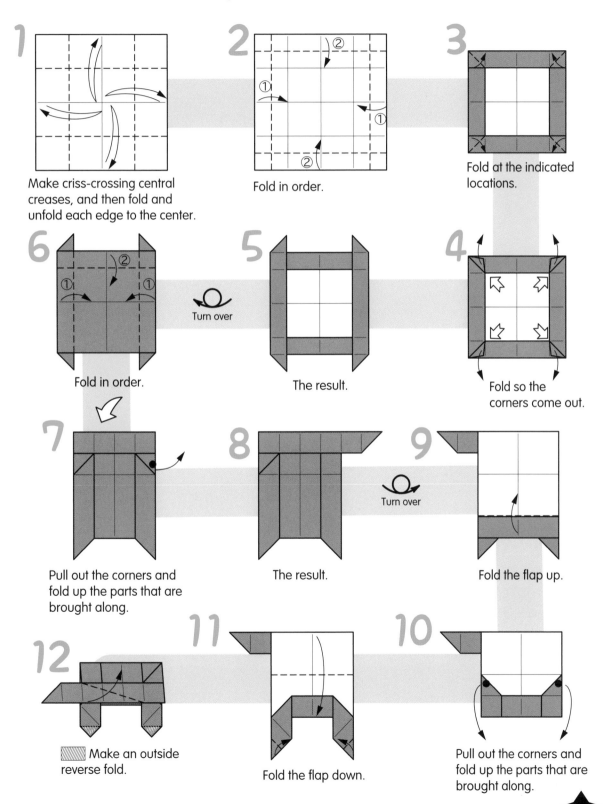

1 Make criss-crossing central creases, and then fold and unfold each edge to the center.

2 Fold in order.

3 Fold at the indicated locations.

4 Fold so the corners come out.

5 The result.

6 Fold in order.

7 Pull out the corners and fold up the parts that are brought along.

8 The result.

9 Fold the flap up.

10 Pull out the corners and fold up the parts that are brought along.

11 Fold the flap down.

12 ▨ Make an outside reverse fold.

Turn over

Turn over

13

Fold the flap up.

14

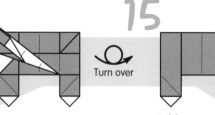

The result.

 Turn over

15

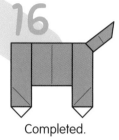

Fold a small portion of the corner behind.

16

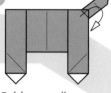

Completed.

All Done!

Face

Body

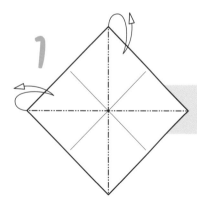

Page 3
2-3 **Apple**

Materials

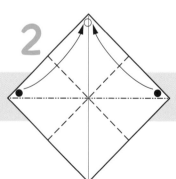

1

Fold in half edge to edge and unfold, both ways. Mountain fold in half corner to corner and unfold, both ways.

2

Collapse the paper along the creases from step 1 so that the filled-circle corners meet the corner with the open circle.

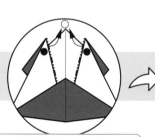

Step 2 in progress

3

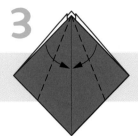

Fold only the top 2 layers.

4

Open pockets and squash them flat.

5

Pinch here and fold up so that the flaps marked with the filled circles meet.

Step 5 in progress

7

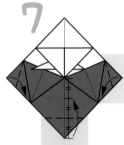

Fold at the indicated locations.

6

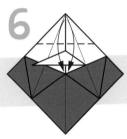

Fold down the top layer only on each side.

8

Insert the tab into the pocket.

9

Open a pocket and squash it flat.

10

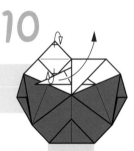

Fold at the indicated locations.

All Done!

Color in

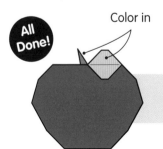

Completed.

12

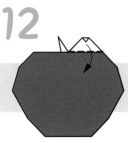

Fold down the top layer only.

Turn over

11

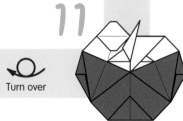

The result.

Elephant

15 Materials		16 Materials	
Face	Body	Face	Body

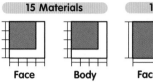
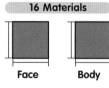

⭐ **Face**

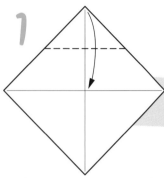

1 Make criss-crossing central diagonal creases, and then fold the top flap to the center.

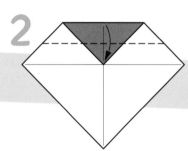

2 Fold the top folded edge to the center.

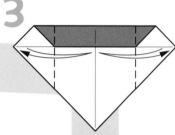

3 Fold the left and right corners to the center. Unfold.

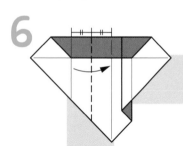

6 Fold the left side in mirror image to steps 4 and 5.

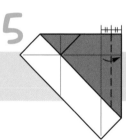

5 Fold so that the crease meets the folded edge.

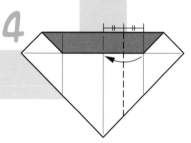

4 Fold, aligning the creases.

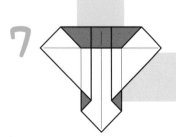

7 The result.

Turn over

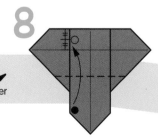

8 Fold so that the filled circle meets the open circle.

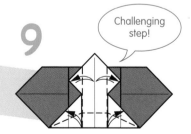

Challenging step!

9 Make creases as shown, and then pinch and fold.

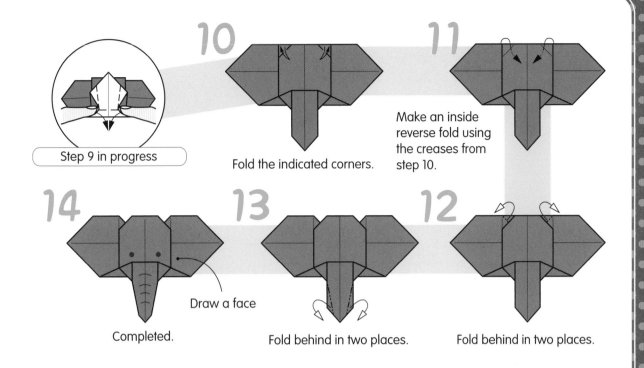

10 Fold the indicated corners.

11 Make an inside reverse fold using the creases from step 10.

Step 9 in progress

12 Fold behind in two places.

13 Fold behind in two places.

14 Completed.

Draw a face

★ Body

From step 4 on page 91

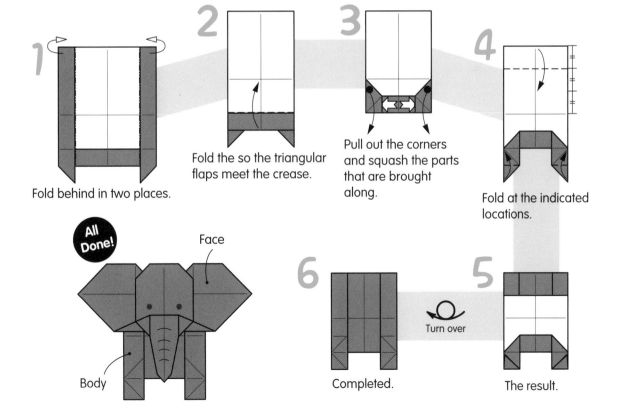

1 Fold behind in two places.

2 Fold the so the triangular flaps meet the crease.

3 Pull out the corners and squash the parts that are brought along.

4 Fold at the indicated locations.

5 The result.

Turn over

6 Completed.

All Done!

Face

Body

Flower

Materials

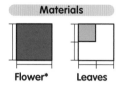

Flower*   Leaves

*Use double-sided origami paper!

★ Flower

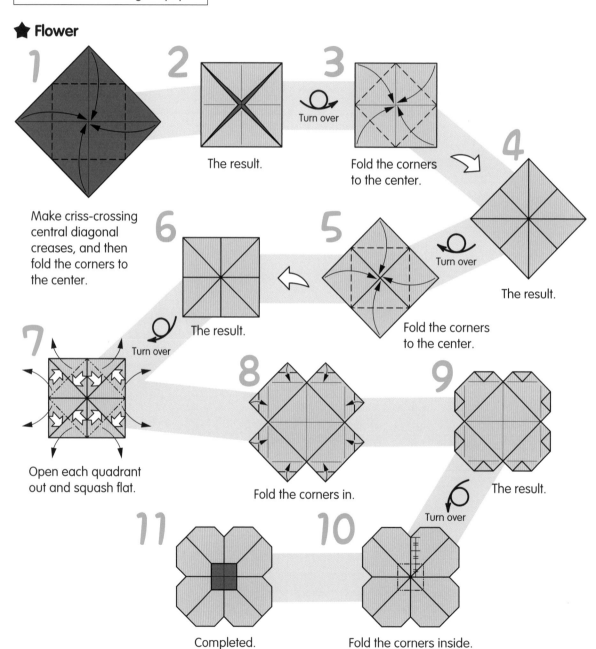

1 Make criss-crossing central diagonal creases, and then fold the corners to the center.

2 The result.

Turn over

3 Fold the corners to the center.

4 The result.

Turn over

5 Fold the corners to the center.

6 The result.

Turn over

7 Open each quadrant out and squash flat.

8 Fold the corners in.

9 The result.

Turn over

10 Fold the corners inside.

11 Completed.

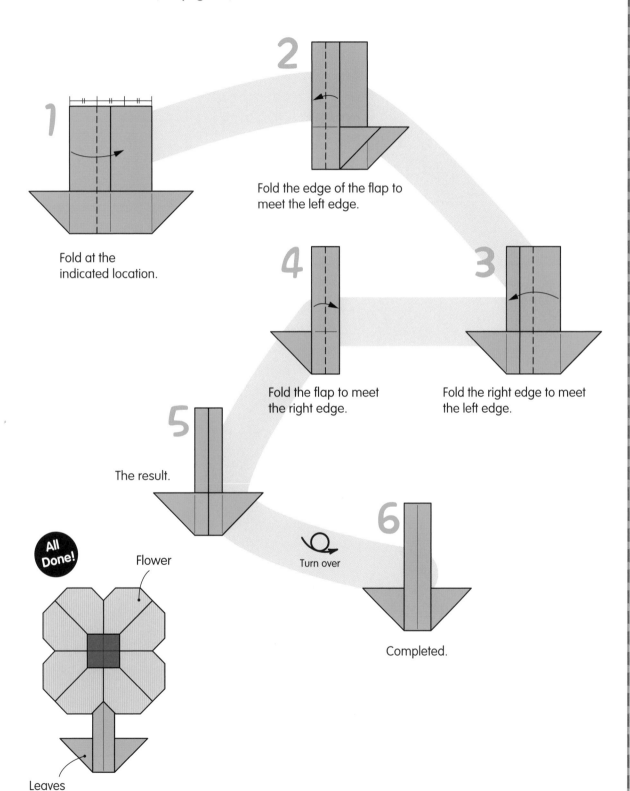

1 Fold at the indicated location.

2 Fold the edge of the flap to meet the left edge.

3 Fold the right edge to meet the left edge.

4 Fold the flap to meet the right edge.

5 The result.

Turn over

6 Completed.

All Done!

Flower

Leaves

Hamburger

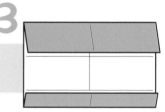

Bun   Filling

⭐ Bun

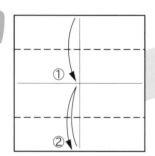

1

① Fold.
② Make a crease.

Make criss-crossing central
creases, and then:
① Fold.
② Make a crease.

2

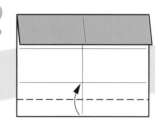

Fold the bottom edge to
the crease made in step 1.

3

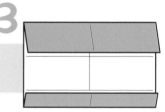

Completed.

⭐ Filling

1

2

3

Make criss-crossing central
creases, and then fold the top
and bottom edges to the center.

Completed.

⭐ Assembly

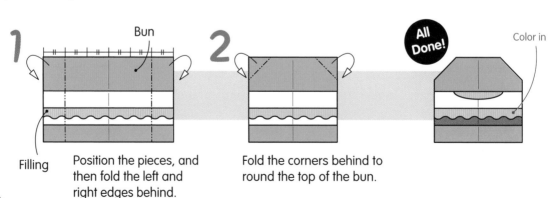

1

Bun

Filling

Position the pieces, and
then fold the left and
right edges behind.

2

Fold the corners behind to
round the top of the bun.

All Done!

Color in

Ice Cream

Materials

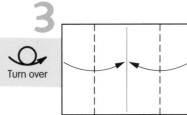

2

The result.

Turn over

3

Fold the left and right edges to the center.

1

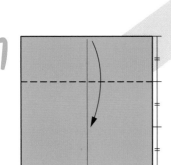

Make a central vertical crease, and then fold down the top flap.

Here, only fold the underlying layer

4

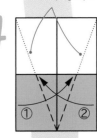

① ②

Fold in order.

6

The result.

Turn over

5

Fold, and then tuck the flap inside the "cone."

Draw a pattern

Completed.

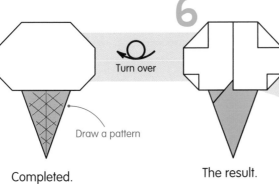

You can stack scoops of ice cream by inserting the cone into the pocket in the ice cream below it

Treasure Chest and Key

⭐ **Key**

1

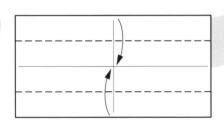

Make criss-crossing central creases, and then fold the top and bottom edges to the center.

2

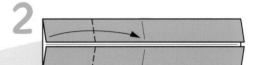

Fold the left edge to the center.

3

The result.

Turn over

5

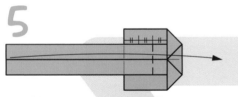

Fold the long rectangular flap to the right.

4

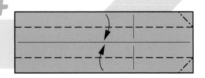

Fold the top and bottom edges, squashing the parts that are brought along into triangles.

6

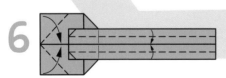

Fold as indicated.

7

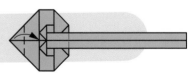

Fold the corner in to the folded edge.

8

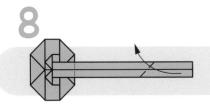

Fold the long rectangular flap up at a 45-degree angle.

9

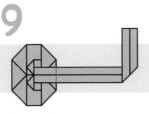

The result.

Rotate

Turn over

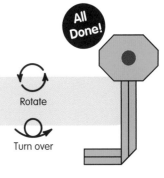

Completed.

★ Treasure chest

1

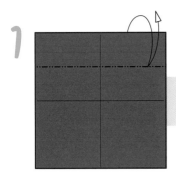

Make criss-crossing central creases, and then install a mountain crease by folding the top edge behind to the center. Unfold.

2

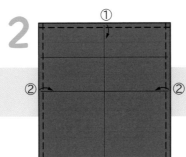

Fold thin strips in order.

3

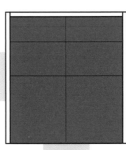

Turn over

4

Fold down along the upper crease line from step 1.

5

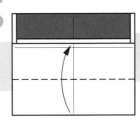

Fold the bottom edge to the folded edge of the flap.

6

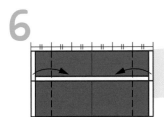

Fold in the outside edges.

7

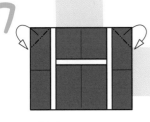

Fold the top corners behind.

All Done!

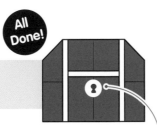

Completed. Draw a keyhole

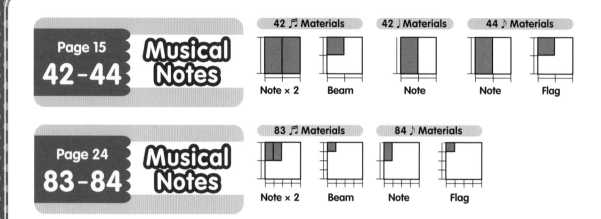

42 🎵 Materials		42 ♩ Materials	44 ♪ Materials	
Note × 2	Beam	Note	Note	Flag

Page 24 83-84	Musical Notes

83 🎵 Materials		84 ♪ Materials	
Note × 2	Beam	Note	Flag

★ ♩ Musical note head and stem

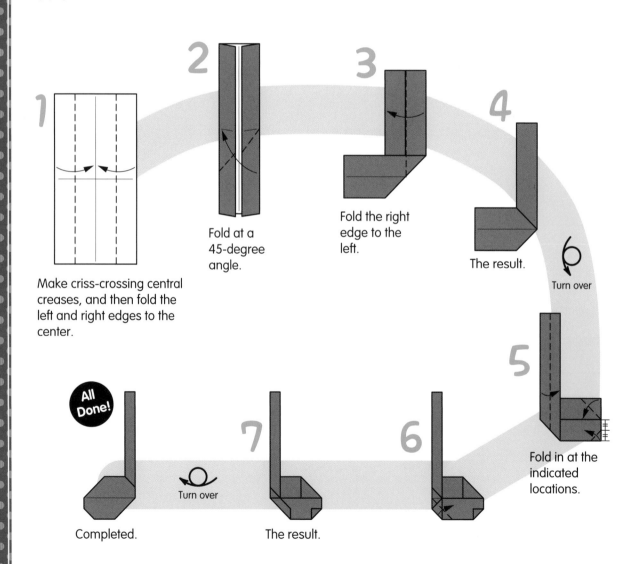

1 Make criss-crossing central creases, and then fold the left and right edges to the center.

2 Fold at a 45-degree angle.

3 Fold the right edge to the left.

4 The result. Turn over

5 Fold in at the indicated locations.

6

7 The result.

All Done! Completed. Turn over

★ ♪ Flag

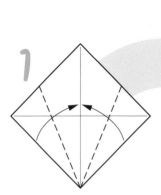

1 Make criss-crossing central diagonal creases, and then fold the bottom edges to the center.

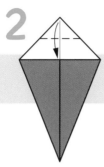

2 Fold down.

3 Fold flaps to the center.

4 Fold in half.

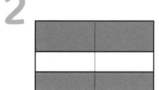

6

5

Completed.

★ ♫ Beam

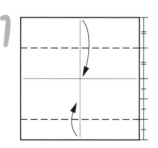

1 Make criss-crossing central creases, and then fold the top and bottom edges to the indicated locations.

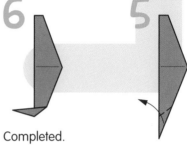

2 Completed.

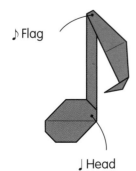

♪ Flag

♩ Head

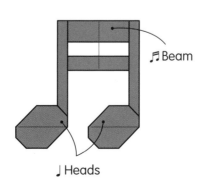

♫ Beam

♩ Heads

Like!

Materials

1

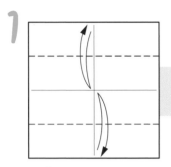

Make criss-crossing central creases, and then make additional horizontal creases.

2

Fold the bottom edge up to the bottom-most crease.

3

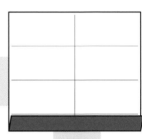

The result.

Turn over

4

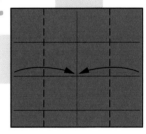

Fold the left and right edges to the center.

5

Fold the left folded edge to the center.

6

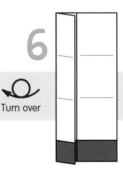

The result.

Turn over

7

Fold the bottom folded edge to the center.

8

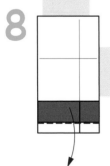

Fold the flap down along the edge of the strip.

9

The result.

Turn over

10

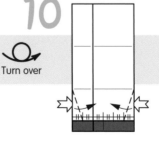

Squash the paper that flares into triangles.

Challenging step!

11

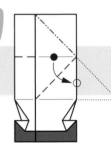

Fold the location marked by the filled circle to the open circle, and squash the paper that flares into a triangle.

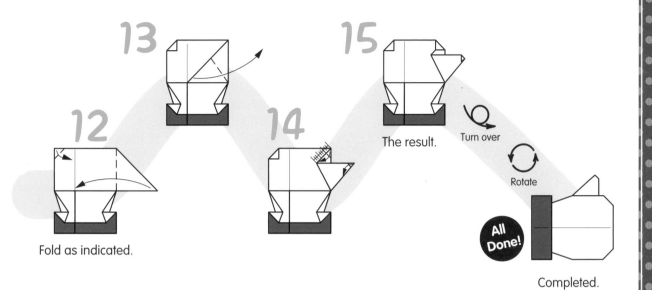

13

12

Fold as indicated.

14

15

The result.

Turn over

Rotate

All Done!

Completed.

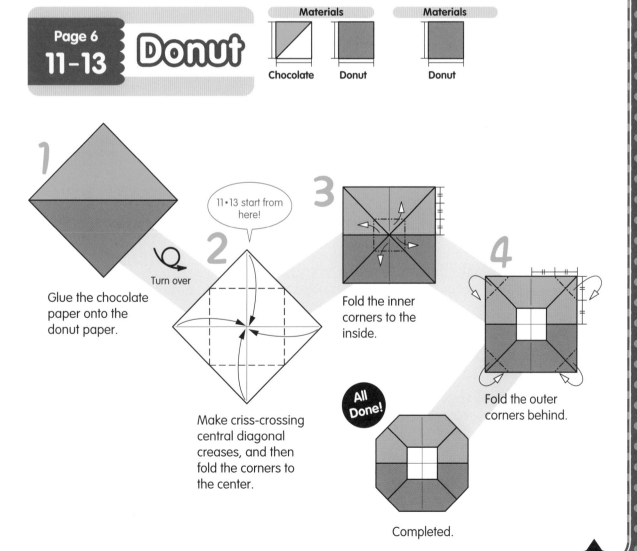

Page 6
11-13 **Donut**

Materials

Chocolate | Donut

Materials

Donut

1

Glue the chocolate paper onto the donut paper.

Turn over

2

11·13 start from here!

Make criss-crossing central diagonal creases, and then fold the corners to the center.

3

Fold the inner corners to the inside.

4

Fold the outer corners behind.

All Done!

Completed.

Ladybug and Clover

★ **Ladybug**

1

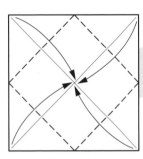

Make criss-crossing central diagonal creases, and then fold the corners to the center.

2

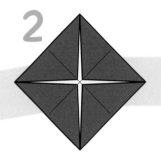

The result.

Turn over

3

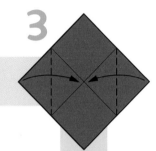

Fold the left and right corners to the center.

6

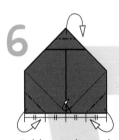

Fold as indicated.

5

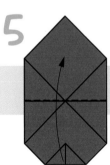

Fold the paper in half on the existing crease.

4

Fold the bottom corner to the indicated position.

7

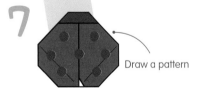

Draw a pattern

Completed.

All Done!

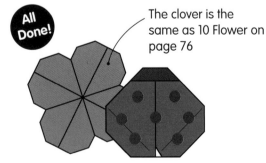

The clover is the same as 10 Flower on page 76

Pencil

Materials

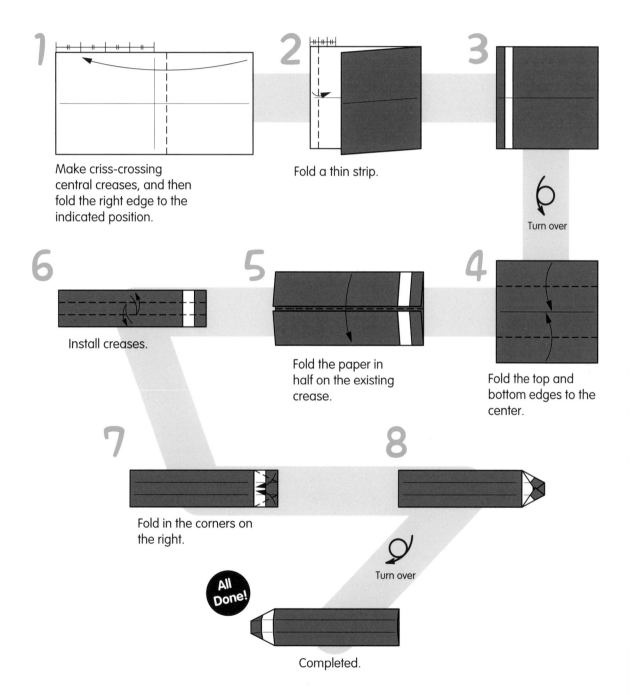

1 Make criss-crossing central creases, and then fold the right edge to the indicated position.

2 Fold a thin strip.

3

Turn over

4 Fold the top and bottom edges to the center.

5 Fold the paper in half on the existing crease.

6 Install creases.

7 Fold in the corners on the right.

8

Turn over

All Done!

Completed.

Page 19 62-63	Crown

Materials

Crown	Ruby

Page 19 65-67	Jewels

Materials

Diamond	Ruby

⭐ **Crown**

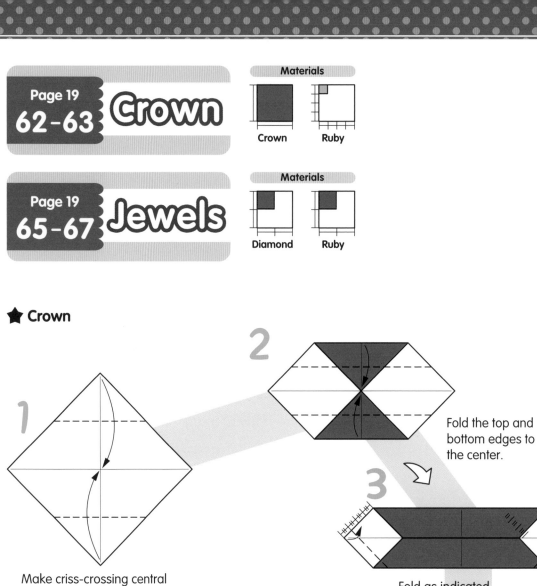

1 Make criss-crossing central diagonal creases, and then fold the top and bottom corners to the center.

2 Fold the top and bottom edges to the center.

3 Fold as indicated.

4

5

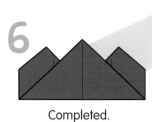

6 Completed.

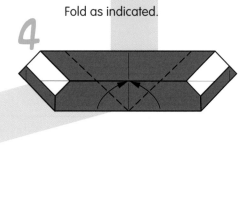

Crown band

Ruby

⭐ Diamond

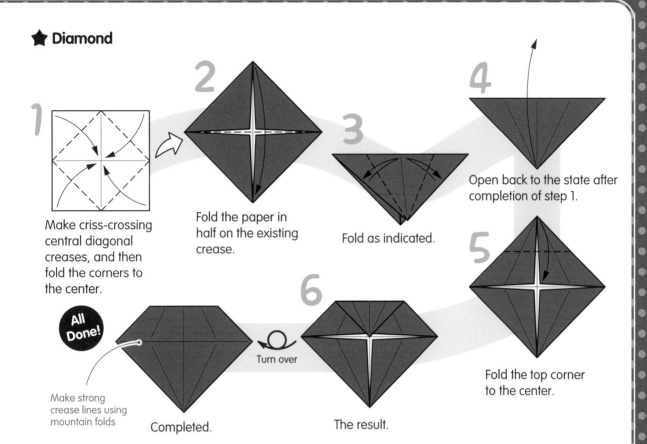

1 Make criss-crossing central diagonal creases, and then fold the corners to the center.

2 Fold the paper in half on the existing crease.

3 Fold as indicated.

4 Open back to the state after completion of step 1.

5 Fold the top corner to the center.

6 The result.

Turn over

All Done! Completed.

Make strong crease lines using mountain folds

⭐ Ruby

Start with a Blintz Base (see page 33)

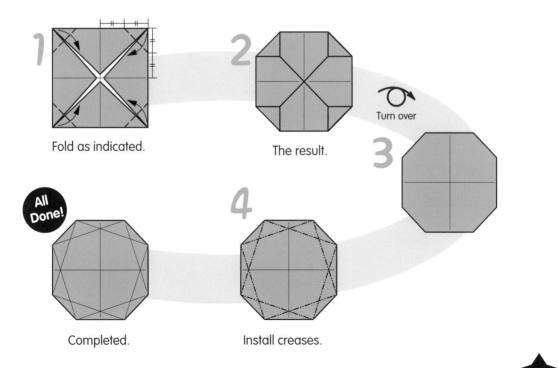

1 Fold as indicated.

2 The result.

Turn over

3

4 Install creases.

All Done! Completed.

Rice Ball

Rice Ball

Rice Bowl

Rice Bowl

★ Rice bowl

1
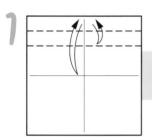
Make criss-crossing central creases, and then make additional horizontal creases.

2
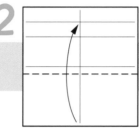
Fold the bottom edge to the top crease.

3
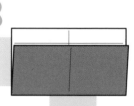
Turn over

4
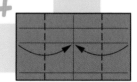
Fold the left and right edges to the center.

5
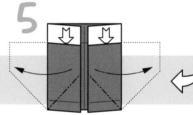
Open out and squash.

6
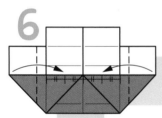
Fold as indicated.

7
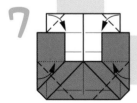

8
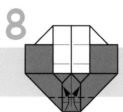

9
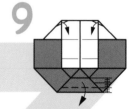

10
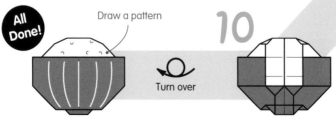
The result.

Turn over

Draw a pattern

All Done!

Completed.

⭐ Rice ball

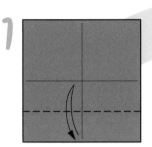

1 Make a cross-shaped crease line and then make a crease line.

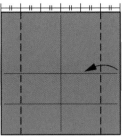
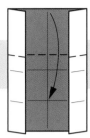
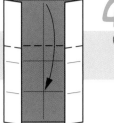

2 Fold as indicated.

3

4
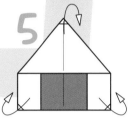

5
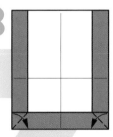

All Done!
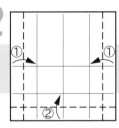
Completed.

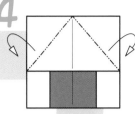

Page 9
21–23

Girl

Materials
Face   Body

⭐ Face

1 Make criss-crossing central creases, and then make additional creases.

2 Fold in order.
① ①
②

3
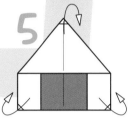
Fold as indicated.

5
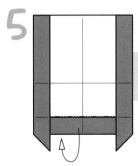

4
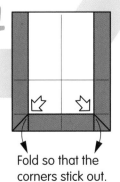
Fold so that the corners stick out.

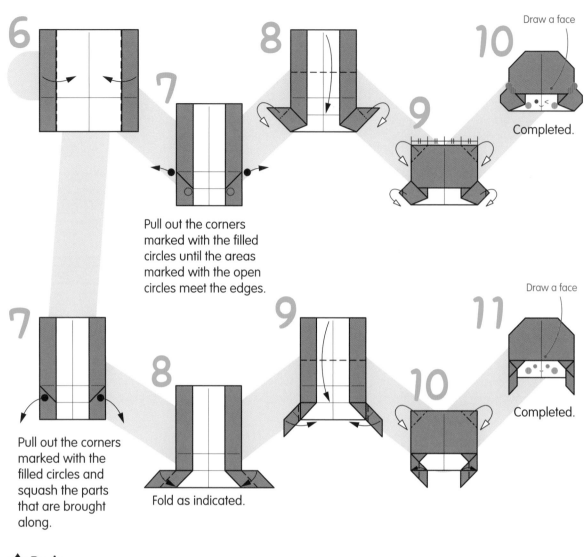

6

7

Pull out the corners marked with the filled circles until the areas marked with the open circles meet the edges.

7

Pull out the corners marked with the filled circles and squash the parts that are brought along.

8

8

Fold as indicated.

9

9

10

Draw a face

Completed.

10

11

Draw a face

Completed.

★ **Body**

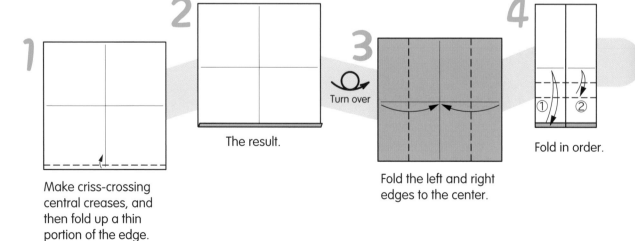

1

Make criss-crossing central creases, and then fold up a thin portion of the edge.

2

The result.

3

Turn over

Fold the left and right edges to the center.

4

① ②

Fold in order.

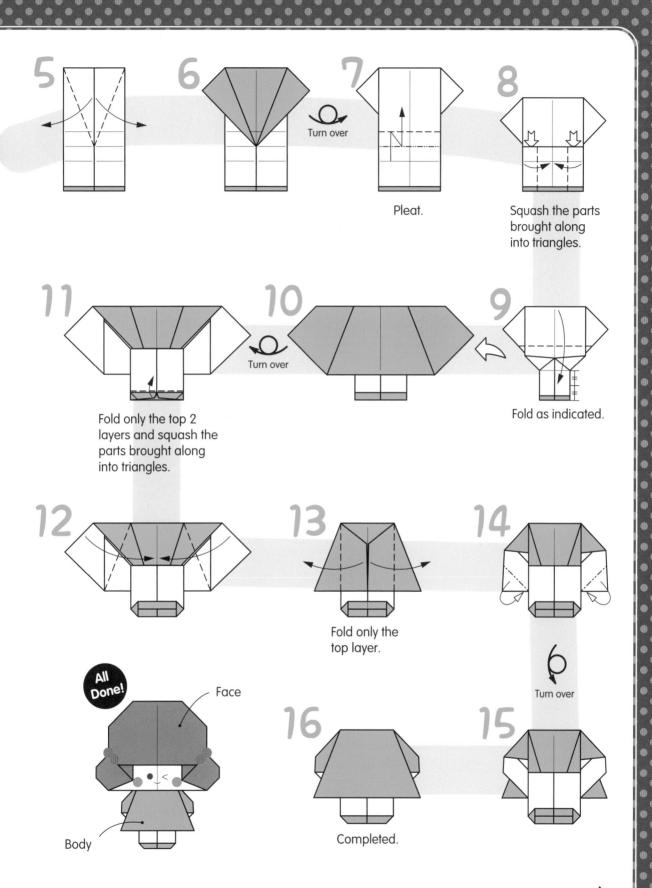

5

6 Turn over

7 Pleat.

8 Squash the parts brought along into triangles.

11 Fold only the top 2 layers and squash the parts brought along into triangles.

10 Turn over

9 Fold as indicated.

12

13 Fold only the top layer.

14

Turn over

All Done!
Face

Body

16 Completed.

15

Page 21
72-73
Strawberry

Page 21
74-75
Sponge Cake

Materials

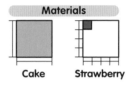

Cake   Strawberry

★ Strawberry

1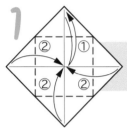

Make criss-crossing central diagonal creases, and then:
① Make a crease.
② Fold.

2

3

Turn over

4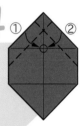

Fold in order so that the edges meet up with the circle.

6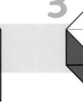

Draw seeds

Completed.

5

★ Cake

1

Make criss-crossing central creases, and then fold and unfold the bottom edge to the center.

2

Fold the bottom edge to the crease.

3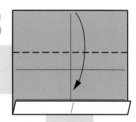

Fold, leaving a small gap.

4

Fold as indicated.

5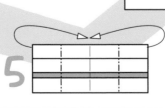

6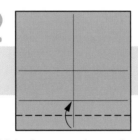

Completed.

All Done!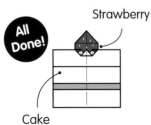

Strawberry

Cake

94

Sign & Bus

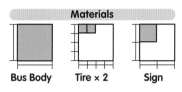
★ Bus body

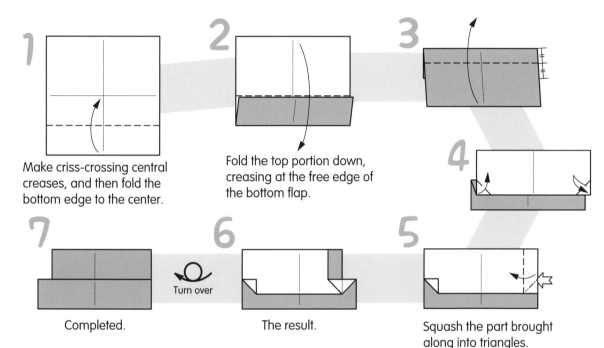

1 Make criss-crossing central creases, and then fold the bottom edge to the center.

2 Fold the top portion down, creasing at the free edge of the bottom flap.

3

4

5 Squash the part brought along into triangles.

6 The result.

Turn over

7 Completed.

★ Tires / Sign

Start with a Blintz Base (see page 33)

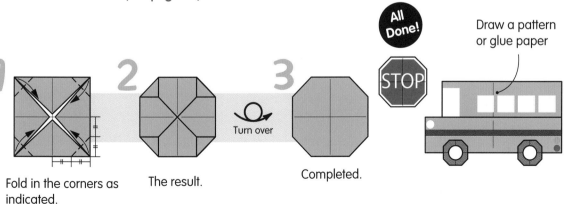

1 Fold in the corners as indicated.

2 The result.

Turn over

3 Completed.

All Done!

Draw a pattern or glue paper

Violin

Materials

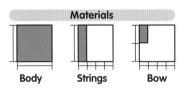

Body   Strings   Bow

⭐ **Body**

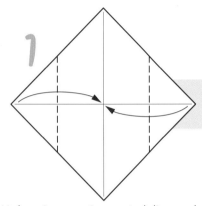

1

Make criss-crossing central diagonal creases, and then fold the left and right corners to the center.

2

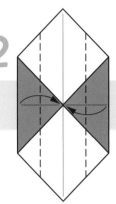

Fold the left and right edges to the center.

3

Fold the top and bottom corner as indicated.

4

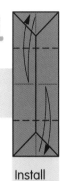

Install creases.

8

Fold as indicated.

7

The result.

6

Pleat in 2 locations, leaving a small gap.

5

The result.

9

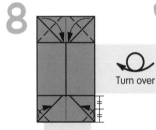

Squash the parts brought along into triangles.

10

The result.

11

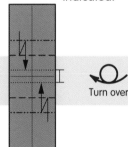

Pinch the corners a little to create a 3D effect.

12

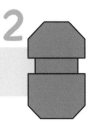

Completed.

★ Bow

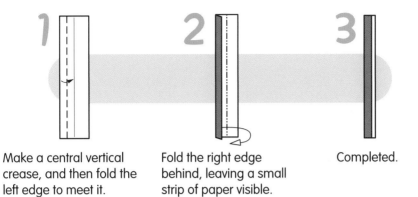

1 Make a central vertical crease, and then fold the left edge to meet it.

2 Fold the right edge behind, leaving a small strip of paper visible.

3 Completed.

★ Strings

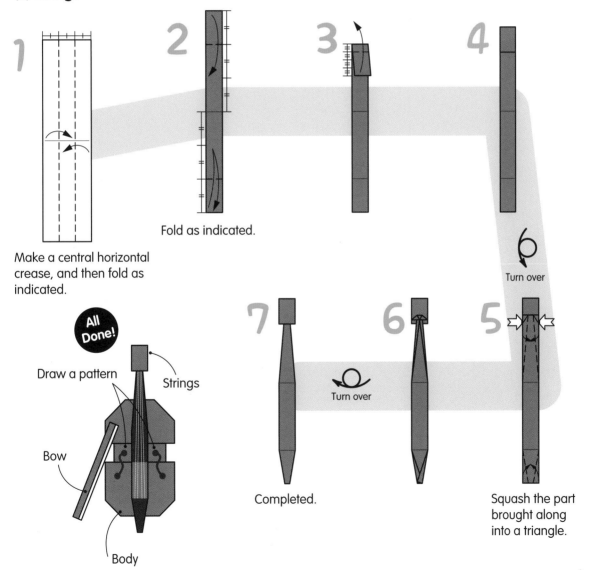

1 Make a central horizontal crease, and then fold as indicated.

2 Fold as indicated.

3

4

Turn over

5 Squash the part brought along into a triangle.

6

Turn over

7 Completed.

All Done!

Draw a pattern

Strings

Bow

Body

 **Orange Juice**

Page 12
31

 **Materials**

Cup   Straw

Page 12
32

Cream Soda

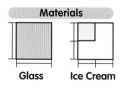 **Materials**

Glass   Ice Cream

Page 12
31

Bubble Tea

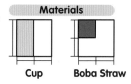 **Materials**

Cup   Boba Straw

★ Cup

1

Make criss-crossing central creases, and then make an additional horizontal crease and a pinch mark.

2

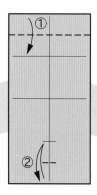

① Fold
② Make a crease line.

3

Fold in at the top and bottom.

4

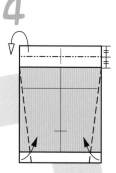

5

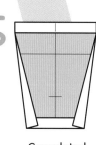

Completed.

★ Straw

1

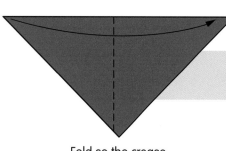

Fold so the crease is slightly off center.

2

Turn over

3

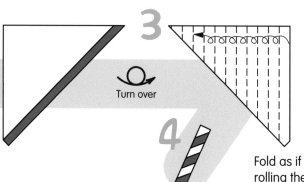

Fold as if rolling the paper.

4

Completed.

98

⭐ Boba straw

Start with a Gatefold (see step 3 of the Boat Base on page 33)

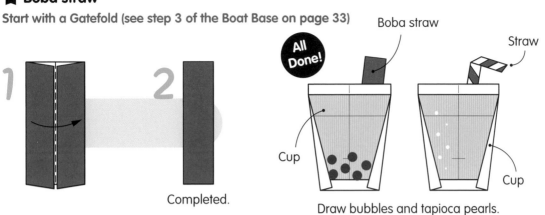

Completed.

All Done!

Boba straw

Straw

Cup

Cup

Draw bubbles and tapioca pearls.

⭐ Glass

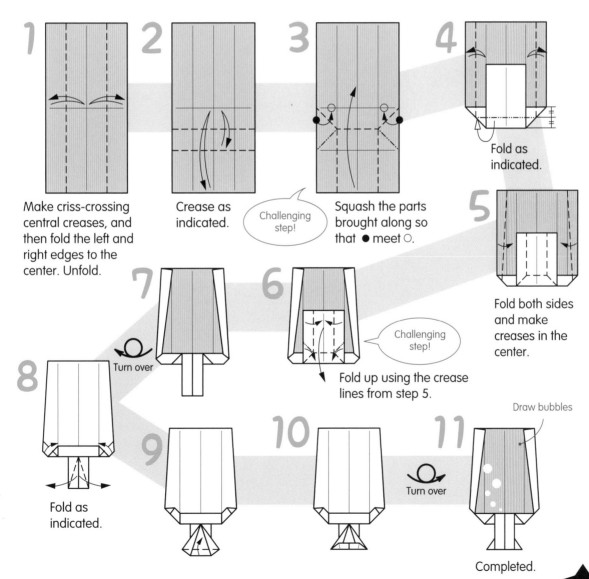

1 Make criss-crossing central creases, and then fold the left and right edges to the center. Unfold.

2 Crease as indicated.

Challenging step!

3 Squash the parts brought along so that ● meet ○.

4 Fold as indicated.

5 Fold both sides and make creases in the center.

Challenging step!

6 Fold up using the crease lines from step 5.

7 Turn over

8 Fold as indicated.

9

10 Turn over

11 Draw bubbles

Completed.

⭐ Ice Cream

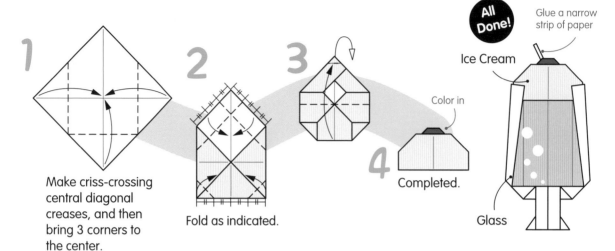

1 Make criss-crossing central diagonal creases, and then bring 3 corners to the center.

2 Fold as indicated.

3

4 Completed.

All Done!

Glue a narrow strip of paper

Ice Cream

Color in

Glass

Page 25 / 87 Wristwatch

Materials

Watch Face   Strap

Page 25 / 88 Smartwatch

Materials

Display   Strap

⭐ Strap

From completed step 2 for the Crown (see page 88)

1 Fold the top and bottom folded edges to the center.

2 Fold the left and right corners as indicated.

3 Make a series of creases at regular intervals (donít make the creases for 88 Smartwatch).

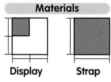
Turn over

4 Completed.

⭐ Watch Face

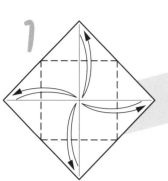

1

Make criss-crossing central diagonal creases, and then fold the corners to the center. Unfold.

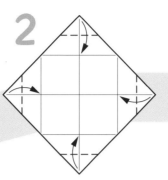

2

3

Fold the folded edges to creases made in step 1.

4

Fold in along existing creases.

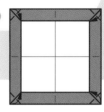

5

Fold the corners in.

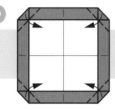

6

Fold the corners in again.

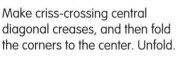

7

Draw the hands and markings

Completed.

⭐ Display*

From completed step 4 (above)

Use double-sided origami paper!

1

Narrow the bezel by folding paper behind.

2

Draw icons

Completed.

All Done!

Strap

Watch Face

Display

Owl

Materials

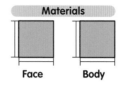

Face   Body

⭐ Face

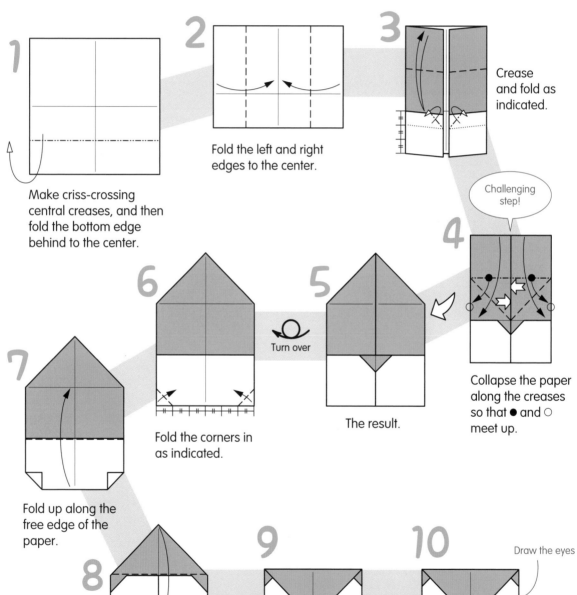

1 Make criss-crossing central creases, and then fold the bottom edge behind to the center.

2 Fold the left and right edges to the center.

3 Crease and fold as indicated.

4 Challenging step!

Collapse the paper along the creases so that ● and ○ meet up.

5 The result.

Turn over

6 Fold the corners in as indicated.

7 Fold up along the free edge of the paper.

8 Fold the top corner to the bottom.

9 Fold the corners behind.

10 Draw the eyes

Completed.

★ Body

1
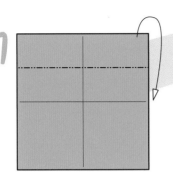
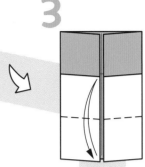

Make criss-crossing central creases, and then fold the top edge behind to the center.

2
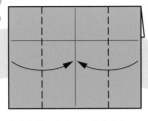

Fold the left and right edges to the center.

3
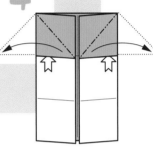

Crease as indicated.

4

Insert your finger to open pockets and then squash on either side.

5
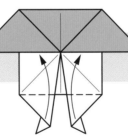

Open out the inside and squash along the crease lines.

6
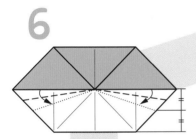

Fold as indicated.

7
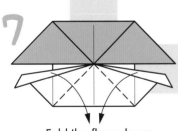

Fold the flaps down on existing creases.

8

Fold the flaps up on existing creases.

9
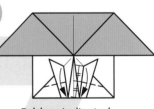

Fold as indicated.

10
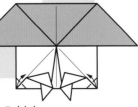

Fold the corners up.

11
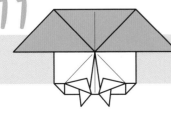

Turn over

Completed.

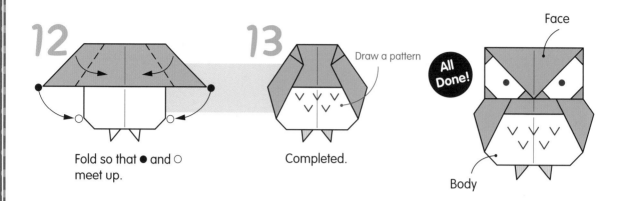

12
Fold so that ● and ○ meet up.

13
Draw a pattern

Completed.

All Done!

Face

Body

Page 26
90-92

Box

Materials

Body*   Ribbon

*Use double-sided origami paper!

⭐ **Box**

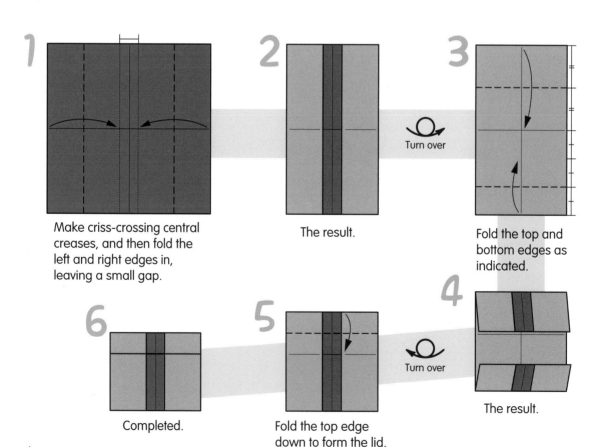

1
Make criss-crossing central creases, and then fold the left and right edges in, leaving a small gap.

2
The result.

Turn over

3
Fold the top and bottom edges as indicated.

4
The result.

Turn over

5
Fold the top edge down to form the lid.

6
Completed.

⭐ Ribbon

From completed step 2 for the Crown (see page 88)

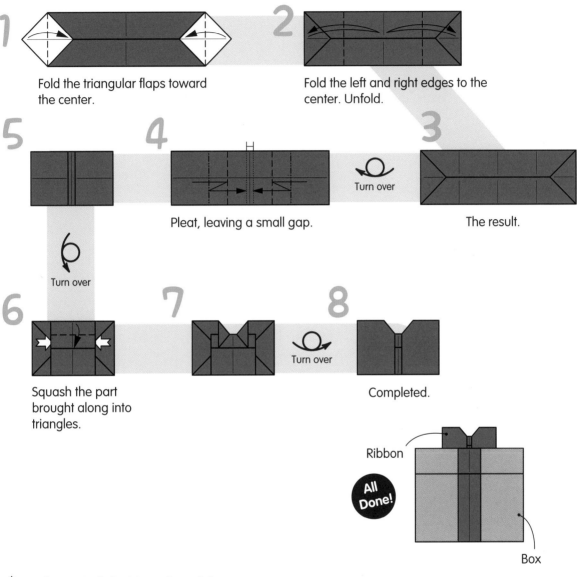

1 Fold the triangular flaps toward the center.

2 Fold the left and right edges to the center. Unfold.

3 Turn over. The result.

4 Pleat, leaving a small gap.

5

6 Turn over. Squash the part brought along into triangles.

7

8 Turn over. Completed.

Ribbon

All Done!

Box

⭐ Make It A Little More Special

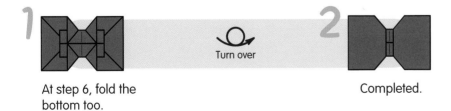

1 At step 6, fold the bottom too.

Turn over.

2 Completed.

Umbrella

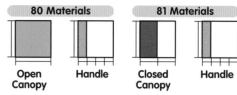

80 Materials		81 Materials	
Open Canopy	Handle	Closed Canopy	Handle

★ Closed Canopy

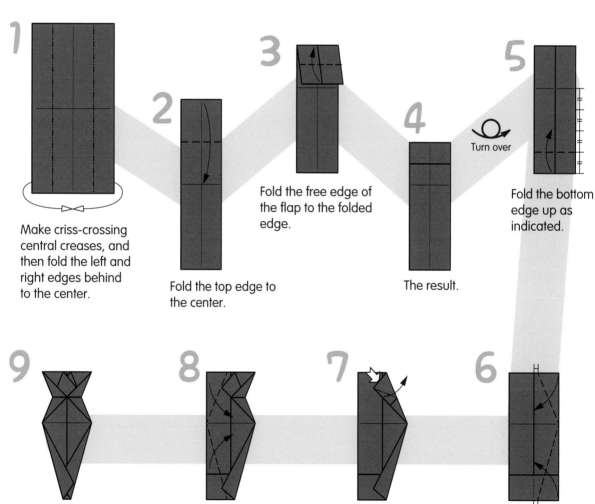

1 Make criss-crossing central creases, and then fold the left and right edges behind to the center.

2 Fold the top edge to the center.

3 Fold the free edge of the flap to the folded edge.

4 The result.

Turn over

5 Fold the bottom edge up as indicated.

6 Fold, leaving a small gap.

7 Open and squash.

8 Fold the left side in mirror image to steps 6 & 7.

9 Completed.

⭐ Open Canopy

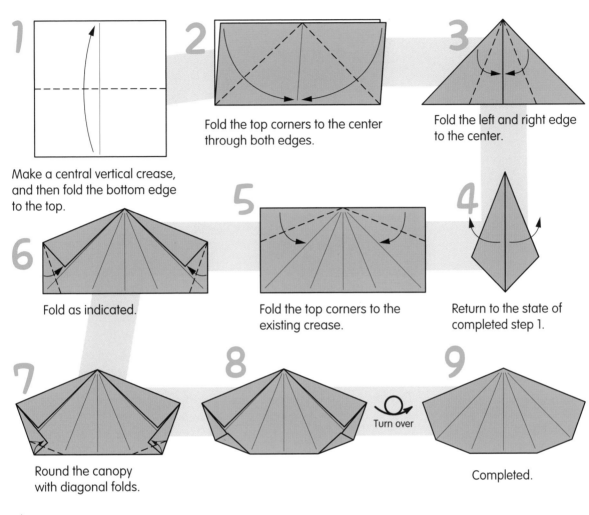

1 Make a central vertical crease, and then fold the bottom edge to the top.

2 Fold the top corners to the center through both edges.

3 Fold the left and right edge to the center.

4 Return to the state of completed step 1.

5 Fold the top corners to the existing crease.

6 Fold as indicated.

7 Round the canopy with diagonal folds.

8 Turn over

9 Completed.

⭐ Handle

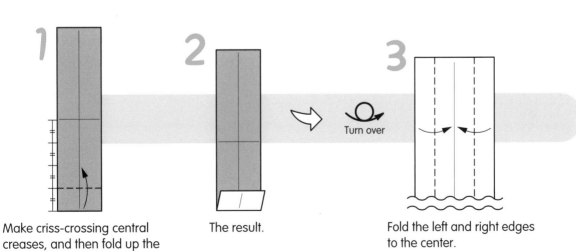

1 Make criss-crossing central creases, and then fold up the bottom edge as indicated.

2 The result.

Turn over

3 Fold the left and right edges to the center.

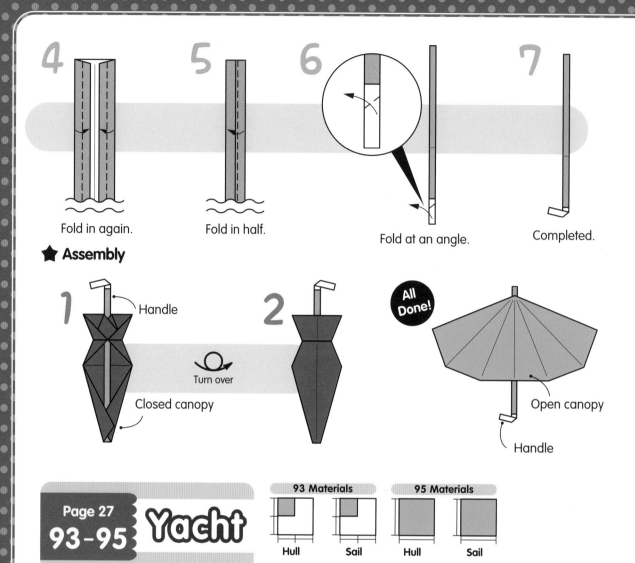

4

Fold in again.

5

Fold in half.

6

Fold at an angle.

7

Completed.

⭐ **Assembly**

1

Handle

Closed canopy

Turn over

2

All Done!

Open canopy

Handle

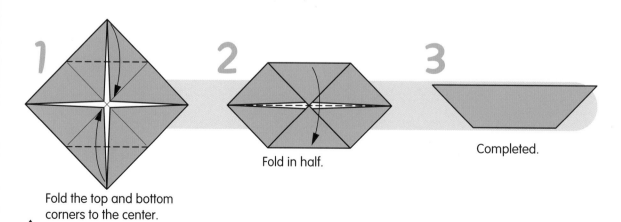

Page 27
93-95 **Yacht**

93 Materials		95 Materials	
Hull	Sail	Hull	Sail

⭐ **Hull**

Start with a Blintz Base (see page 33)

1

Fold the top and bottom corners to the center.

2

Fold in half.

3

Completed.

★ Sail

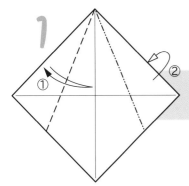

1

Make criss-crossing central diagonal creases, and then crease and fold in order.

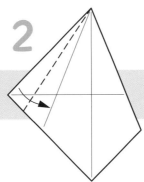

2

Fold the top left edge to the existing crease.

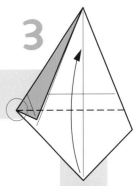

3

Fold so the horizontal crease terminates at the circled location.

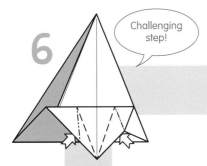

6

Challenging step!

Make narrow folds and squash the parts brought along into triangles.

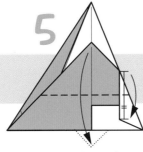

5

Fold as indicated.

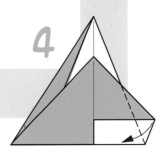

4

Fold in the projecting flap.

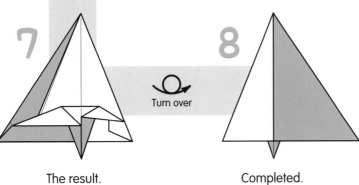

7

The result.

Turn over

8

Completed.

All Done!

Sail

Hull

Zebra

 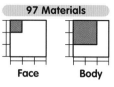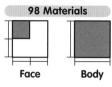
⭐ **Face**

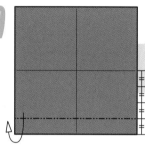

1 Make criss-crossing central creases, and then fold the bottom edge behind as indicated.

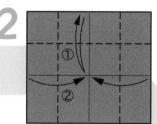

2
① Make a crease line.
② Fold.

3
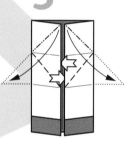
Open out the inside and squash along the crease lines.

4
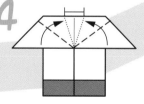
Fold, leaving a gap.

5
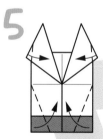
Fold as indicated.

6

The result.

Turn over

7
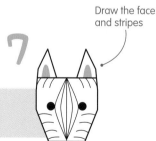
Draw the face and stripes

Completed.

⭐ Body

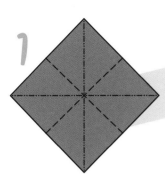

1 Fold in half edge to edge and unfold, both ways. Mountain fold in half corner to corner and unfold, both ways.

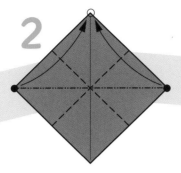

2 Collapse the paper along the creases from step 1 so that the filled-circle corners meet the corner with the open circle.

3 Make crease lines on only the top 2 layers.

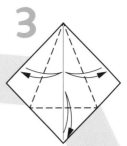

4 Fold the top layer narrowly as if rolling.

5 Open out only the top layer and fold up along the crease lines.

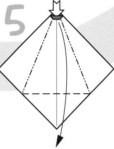

6 Fold the opposite side in the same way as in steps 3-5.

7 Turn over 1 layer in front, and 1 behind.

8 Fold only the top layer.

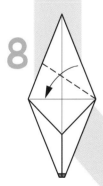

9 Narrow the flap.

10 Turn over

11

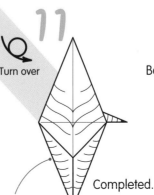

Draw stripes

Completed.

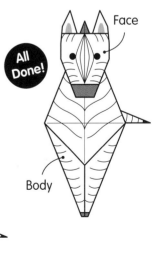

All Done!

Face

Body

Tree

Materials

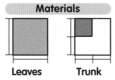

Leaves   Trunk

⭐ Leaves

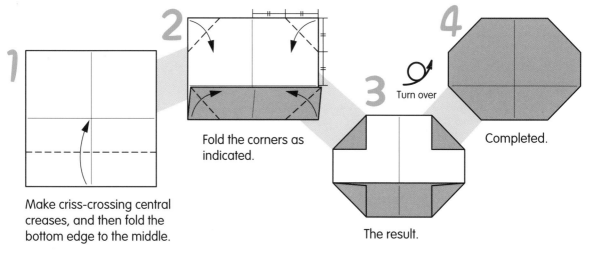

1 Make criss-crossing central creases, and then fold the bottom edge to the middle.

2 Fold the corners as indicated.

3 Turn over

The result.

4 Completed.

⭐ Trunk

Start from step 7 of the Boat Base (see page 33)

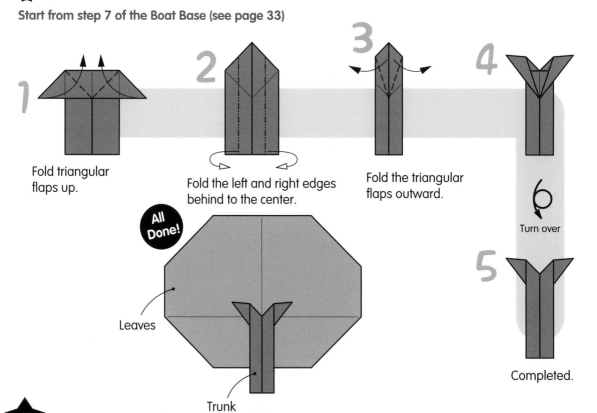

1 Fold triangular flaps up.

2 Fold the left and right edges behind to the center.

3 Fold the triangular flaps outward.

4 Turn over

5 Completed.

All Done!

Leaves

Trunk